From Ex to Next!

An Empowered Woman's Guide to Dating Again

By Kim Hess and Michael Masters

Published by Michael Masters and Kim Hess

Copyright 2010 Masters Hess

ISBN-13: 978-1461036388
ISBN-10: 1461036380

Table of Contents

All 9 of our videos can be found here
http://www.startdatingagain.net/?page_id=22

Preface

This book was created on the floor of Kim's Apartment in San Francisco with copious amounts of coffee. We banged away at our computers till the wee hours of the morning, and during the occasional break we started to piece together what we really wanted readers to get out of the book. First we thought we would do the shotgun approach and create the war and peace of dating books but fortunately for everyone this was abandoned.

Instead, we decided to make the book multimedia, a little more fun and from the hip. We decided to discuss more difficult/specific topics over video, which you may very well need addressed in the greater detail we do. Also, since we are both bloggers we have included some relevant stories in the right places, not to bulk up the book but to drive certain points home. These stories are in italics and although are not necessary to get your butt back in the dating world, they are helpful and entertaining, it is up to if you would like to include them in your experience of the book.

Since our book has two voices initially we had Kim's voice in red and mine black. When the book was moved to the Kindle and then to black and white print, I realized this wouldn't work so Kim's voice will be slightly lighter in intensity and a different font. Hopefully this is clear to everyone reading.

3

Lastly, when I read a non-fiction book I generally don't start at the beginning since much of the information may not be applicable to me. We are totally OK with you doing the same; all of the chapters can stand on their own if need be. While we would like you to read the entire book, if you for example, are not in the grieving process any longer the first section may not be that valuable to you. Please feel free to skip it and jump into what will really make a difference in your life.

Thanks for reading,
Mike and Kim
backintherelationshipgame@gmail.com

P.S. I swear a lot, sorry about that – Mike

Introduction – Why we can help you

My divorce completely rocked my world, and not in a good way, like having great sex or finding the perfect cream cheese danish. No, my world was rocked by the sudden fear that I would never be loved again.

I fell in love with a man and committed to him happily, never imagining that one day we would no longer be in a relationship filled with love, sex, and nice words. No one gets married thinking they're going to get divorced. No one gets into a relationship thinking of breaking up. But it happens every day. All the time. Women who once thought that the rest of their life would always include a loving husband/partner are having rude awakenings. Sometimes-no, but MOST times-there are no happily-ever-afters. A heart gets broken, love fades, you realize you can't even stand the way he brushes his teeth! Whatever it is, your happily ever after retreats into the nothingness by which it came and you're left just trying to be happy.

How does a woman get back being happy when trying to get over divorce or a breakup? With support, kind words, and sometimes tequila. But mainly with the hope and faith that she is a wonderful person, a beautiful person who has to accept the facts and keep going.

I am **Kim Hess** the divorce guru. As a divorce guru I help people realize that their lives can be better after a divorce or breakup than it was before. "Is this possible?" they wonder. Can someone's life get back to normal, let alone be *happier* after dealing with the horrible repercussions of a divorce or breakup?

(The main repercussion being your neighborhood dry cleaning lady asking when you're going to get married again every time you take in a stained dress!)

I'm here to tell you that yes; you can be happy, happier, (happiest!) after the man you thought you'd be with forever is gone. I am living proof. My life is grand, and it would not be so if I were still tethered (yeah, I said tethered as in chained, held down) by my then husband. One significant way to be happier and more confident is to eventually get back out there and see what the world has to offer you in terms of fabulous men. Relationships are like swimsuits: you gotta try a heck of a lot on before you find the one that is fabulous! Enter the Master Dater!

Mike the Master Dater is my go to guy when I'm on my dating adventures (and oh, what adventures I have!) When my confidence is low, I call Mike. When I don't know if a guy is just after sex, I call Mike. When I wonder if a guy is too clingy and tells me he wants to marry me on the first date and have 15 biological children…well I run screaming from the date *then* call Mike to find out why the hell I attracted that weirdo!

I met Mike when I was new to dating and new to being a divorce guru. I had the guru thing down pat…the dating thing…not so much. I interviewed Mike for my radio show aptly named Divorce Guru, and spent the whole interview asking him questions about MY dating life instead of answering the audience's questions. My dating savior was born.

Mike is a great guy that has actually been through his own heartaches, and roller coaster ride of love. More importantly, Mike knows women and what we should and should not be doing in the dating world. And, the best part of all: he's straight! So he ALWAYS knows what my dates (who are straight men) are thinking or planning (or most likely, NOT thinking, and NOT planning!)

So, you've got a Divorce Guru and a Master Dater who are here by your side to help you navigate the treacherous but crazy fun waters of dating. We're here to help move from Ex to Next as smoothly as possible. What more could you want? Oh, yeah, I guess a man! Read on and we'll show you how it's done.
– Kim Hess

I am **Mike Masters** I have never been married so I obviously have never been divorced but I understand relationships like Tiger Woods does blond hookers. (Yeah ladies, Mike's that good!) I have been in the trenches, in pain and suffering to the degree that I have considered removing myself permanently from the equation, seriously.

I think most of us have been to this point where we believe there will be no end to our suffering. Having been so emotionally hurt that your heart may physically hurt and believing that there is no way you can ever love again.

Granted, I may not know exactly the pain you are going through because I haven't been in a relationship for 5/10/15 years and have it come crashing down around me. I do know the pain of losing love. However, that is not what our book is about, it is about moving on and getting your dating life back on track.

Learning that things are really not that bad and good feelings and good men are right around the corner. And I want to teach you how to be that empowered, happy, hot, sexy, diva, so your ex will curse the day that he ever did anything that got on your nerves!

There is a mourning period after death and the end of a committed long-term relationship and not going through

7

this seriously compromises your future choices. However, I believe that many of us revel in our unhappiness. We remain as a victim as long as possible so that we don't have to make the painful venture into the unknown to find happiness again.

Kim and I will help you to move on as quickly (and as healthily) as possible to the next stage. We want to help you find the happiness that is only just around the corner. We want to hold your hand along the way so that you feel safe starting life over again after a breakup or divorce.

We also want to slap you on the ass, fluff up your hair and push you out into the world that's just waiting for you with open arms, and yell "You go girl!" as loud as we can to encourage, motivate, and support you!

-Mike Masters http://www.mikethemasterdater.com
-Kim Hess Divorce Guru http://www.KimHess.com

Part one: Moving on

I. Moving on - Are you ready to date again?

Are you ready to date again?

Okay. It's happening. You've made the decision. Or the decision's been made for you. You are no longer in a committed relationship. No husband, no boyfriend. You're a single woman now. You've joined the Broken Hearts Club. Everyone's broken up. Everyone's been hurt. The break up talk has happened, the divorce papers have been filed, the tears have been cried, he's moved out or his stuff is gone from your place. And you are fast on your way to becoming a single woman, again. But are you entirely comfortable being a single woman? Is it appropriate to date yet? Are you ready to jump back into the dating pool?

Oh, the legality of it all!

First things first, are you technically divorced or ready to date yet? You may wonder if this matters. For me, it didn't matter. I started dating while I was legally separated from my soon to be ex husband. The divorce papers had been served, documents were filed, we had been to court several times, and had already established joint visitation and custody for our two sons. My marriage was over. My soon to be ex started dating before the papers were filed.

Hell, he had been dating other women (and maybe some men) two years before we had even talked about divorce! I believed I was well within my right to start dating, seeing he was out there, and having fun. In some states there is a mandatory "waiting period" of 6 months or more before a divorce can become final. I'm guessing the courts are hoping you will change your mind and decide to stay married. Yeah, right. Or maybe they don't want to get to work on giving you your freedom…either way sometimes you have to wait several months before you are officially divorced. In some cases years! I can personally attest to that. I filed my divorce papers in October of 2007. My divorce became final and official December of 2009. Over 2 years! Should I have waited over 2 years to dip my toes into the dating pool? Some would say yes.

If you are strongly religious and abide by all of the rules and codes of morality then it's probably a good idea for you to wait. Religious shame and guilt can be rough when trying to get your groove on as a single woman.

I receive a daily encouraging email for 365 days from an organization called Divorce Care. They make no bones about pushing the whole morality button in their work in helping people get through divorce. I was desperate for help and guidance, so I was willing to get help no matter what source it came from. Here is the "quiz" they offer to us going through divorce and contemplating dating:

A Quiz
Day 179

In this multiple-choice quiz, choose one of the following: (a) married or (b)
single.

1. What are you the day before you get married?

2. What are you the day before you have your final divorce decree in hand?

3. What are you the day after you have your final divorce decree in hand?

The answers are b, a, and b. The first answer is easy. The second answer is
tricky because you may feel single at that point, even though you are not. The
third answer is also difficult because you may still feel married because you
have been in that state for so long.

"If you are still married, you are not available to date," says Sabrina Black.
"Even though you feel emotionally divorced from the person, you are still married by law and by God's standards.

When I received this I looked it over, said out loud, "hmm, good point" and then deleted it. Some will say that your marriage is more than a piece of paper. I've even heard that you wouldn't drive around town illegally without a driver's license so why date if you are legally still married to your husband.

What do I say to those people? Horse shit! They're right: marriage is more than a piece a paper. It is a relationship, a bond, a commitment between two people that is emotional, spiritual, financial, and physical. Once one or all of these components are broken and the commitment to each other is broken, then in my brilliant mind, a marriage no longer exists.

You're telling me if your husband tells you he's going to love and respect you forever, then goes out and sleeps with a hooker, a sheep, and an inflatable doll (well the inflatable doll might get a pass) that YOU have to be punished by waiting for the legal system to give you the stamp of approval that you are now a single woman?

The Divorce Police

11

Can I let you in on something? There IS no divorce police. You heard me. No one is going to chase you down, handcuff you, and throw you in jail if you decide to date before your divorce is final or your breakup has reached an "acceptable" time period. It's like wearing white after Labor Day. If you're a woman, you know what I'm talking about! In the past, one would be ridiculed or laughed at for wearing white shoes past September. So just like it used to be taboo to wear white after Labor Day, it used to be taboo to date before your divorce was final. Or date "too soon" before a respectable amount of time has passed when you've broken up from a long-term relationship.

Thank heavens times are a changing. You can wear white after Labor Day and no one cares. And really, why should they. It's none of their business what you're wearing or the color. Just like it's no ones business when you start to date again. Ask yourself: am I ready to get back in the game? If the answer is yes, it's yes. Remember, there are no divorce police!

However, I don't recommend getting into a full-fledged relationship if you haven't fully recovered. I feel that marriage is much more than the legal component. It is definitely emotional, mental and physical. In my opinion once it has been decided that divorce is the next course of action and there is no going back then I am no longer married to this person in my heart. Legally: yes. Emotionally, physically, and mentally: no. Only you can decide how you feel about this topic. You may have your friends, and family state that you can go one way or another but in your heart you know what you feel is right. But I need to reiterate that it's no one's business but your own!

Moving on from the Ex

Whoever you date and bring into your life, is going to be new and shiny. You can't help but to make comparisons to him and your soon to be ex, which isn't fair. You have no major history or emotional ties (or mortgage payments, or dealing with the mold problem in the bathroom) so the new relationship will seem perfect…for a while at least. Plus, it's easy to want to seek refuge in someone, anyone, while you are still recovering from the emotional pain of this break up. It leaves you less time to cry and ruminate on your part in the divorce or breakup. Face it; nice dinners, and great (or even so-so) sex can be like a drug, which numbs your heart and mind to the pain. A fun drug, but a drug nonetheless. And we all know what your brain looks like on drugs.

There are some very valid points in not dating and waiting until the divorce is legally final. It gives you time to recover. The, "you're going to die and go to hell" preachers I grew up with will advocate that this is what God and the Pope would want. I advocate that you should do what is best for you… Which is probably taking at least a year before jumping into the dating pool.

So what about my friend Gail who was emotionally far gone from her husband and was DYING to start dating again even before the divorce was final? Hell, she hadn't had sex in over a year and wanted to get back in the game as fast as possible! You would really tell her to wait a year??

If I had a nickel for every time I heard a woman going through a divorce/breakup say, "I'm ready to date, I was done with that relationship years ago" I'd have Oprah money by now!

You won't believe what we women with broken hearts and broken dreams will say to make everything appear okay. We want to feel like we're not hurting and we want the world around us to see how this breakup is not hurting us. So what do we say? "I'm ready to date!" Do you know why your friend

13

and a lot of other women are chaffing at the bit to get out and date? We want to appear strong and happy about ourselves while invalidating the relationship we had. This way we won't feel like a big fat failure which is what most of us think when a marriage/relationship doesn't last until "death do us part."

When we jump into dating too soon we also want to replace the feelings we had when we were in a loving relationship. Hell, we want to *replace* that relationship and NOW. If you have lived with a man, loved a man with all your being, maybe pushed out his offspring, planned to nurture and have wrinkly old people sex with said man until he (notice I said *he* not *you*!) died, you need time to mourn.

Mourn Girl Mourn

Gotta tell ya, it's impossible to mourn if you have "left the relationship years ago" but still live with him, eat dinner with him, pick up his dry cleaning and still hold the role of wife/partner. The healing begins when it's declared. When you declare (and better yet announce it from hilltops) that you and he are no longer a couple, that's when it's real. I have clients that have not had sex with their husbands/partners in 5 years but when it comes time to sever the marriage/relationship and move out they fall apart wondering what they will do without him.

You probably are excited to get out there and date just like Mike's friend Gail. Just like I was. I was thinking, "So many beautiful men, and so little time!" Until Gail and her husband are in separate homes, living separate lives and processed the loss she is going through, I guarantee she will be on the bathroom floor crying wondering how she got to the point that she no longer has a man that loves her. Been there, done that. We all have, and I'm here to tell you, you'll get through it. Please understand, you can't skip this crucial step in mourning

14

and jump to the place of gleefully having great sex with a man who adores you but this will come in time.

No Shortcuts to Healing

While going through the divorce process you can't take a shortcut that's going to lead you to the point where you were happy and at peace like when you were happily committed (I'm assuming at some point you were happily committed!) Any shortcut you think you're taking...like, oh, I don't know, dating and falling in love with the guy who has taken you out to dinner once, slept with you and only calls you after midnight for sex... that shortcut is not going to lead to confidence, peace, and contentment with oneself, or self fulfillment. It's going to lead you full circle to the reason you are getting divorced in the first place. Think carefully about why you want to date. Here are the most common reasons women have:

Companionship

- Do you want a buddy to go to dinner and the movies with on the weekends?
- Hot sex without attachment?
- Find dating and the opposite sex fun but not trying to make it your whole world, or the reason you get out of bed in the morning.

These are valid reasons to want to date. You want someone to have fun with, someone to chill with, and men are ever so dreamy! You want to start dating because it's fun, but you're not ready to jump into the whole monogamy thing without getting yourself straightened out first.

Fulfillment

- Is it to find long-term companionship because what's a woman without a man?
- There is no way you can ever spend Friday or Saturday night alone without a built in date?
- Trying to replace your ex?
- Don't like being alone?
- Do you need validation from the opposite sex?
- Boost in self-esteem?
- Someone to raise your 5 children by 5 different men?

These are NOT valid reasons to want to date soon after a breakup or divorce. These are not valid reasons to date EVER! If you had an inkling that some (or all) of these reasons pertain to you…well, we got some work to do. And that work entails enforcing the belief that you are wonderful and special and don't need outside validation to feel okay about yourself. You are enough. And once you realize you're enough and "all that", then the man who is worthy of one who is "all that" will come knockin' on your door. Well, not literally but you get what I mean.

I know most people try to jump into dating to recover what their divorce or break up has snatched away. What is gone from your last relationship cannot be magically reproduced like bunnies in a magician's hat. What can be reproduced is your self-esteem and love that you once had for yourself. Replacing heartache with heartache just ain't healthy girl! But replacing heartache with loving yourself…well that's priceless AND will attract you a darn good man. Which is what you want, right?

Okay, I fundamentally agree with you Kim but this really is not reality. As a former nutritionist teaching weight loss, I can tell you that NOBODY actually follows what I

16

tell them to do. Rather they mess up, they fall down, they cheat but with support they ultimately make it to their goals. I would guess that you are so passionate about this because it is a trap you fell into as well. I say lets prepare people for when and where they fall down.

Time heals

This last Christmas I experienced something that shook me up, although it was a bit silly. My stepmother gave my brother-in-law a stocking stuffer that was a cute little rubber chicken. When you squeezed the chicken it ejected a cute little ball of thin rubber out of its backside. While the room laughed I was instantly brought to tears. This little toy reminded me of how my pet parrot of 18 years died in my arms. She had problems with her insides and would eject her intestines every time she went to the bathroom. I hadn't thought about this in years.

I left the room, dried my eyes and it dissipated within minutes. I didn't really feel much pain it was more the shocking accuracy of the toy. As I quickly got myself back under control I realized that I really had healed 99% from the traumatic loss of my childhood pet. When she took her last breath in my arms and her little head lulled to the side, I have never felt such sadness. However, I naturally healed from this injury because I knew that I did my best with what I had. I knew that it was not my fault she died, and the process of time did its work.

You did the best you could with the tools and training you were given. It was not your fault that things didn't work out, and to dwell on this, to not forgive him or yourself is counterproductive. It is going to hurt, it is

17

going to suck but this too will pass as long as you remove the barriers to healing. Constantly picking at a wound, not only will halt it's healing but it will scar, and that scar will radically hinder you from your next successful relationship.

Supplemental Video: How long to wait to date?
http://www.startdatingagain.net/?page_id=64
How long should you wait to date? While this is very personal Kim and I will help you decide what is best for you.

Need a little more encouragement? Here is how my mother helped me move on.

Move on after divorce...it can be done
By Kim Hess

Since you're reading this I'm assuming you need to move on after divorce. Or you're some sort of sadist that gets some weird pleasure from knowing that other people are trying to move past a painful event in their lives. If you're one of the latter, oh, you'll get yours buddy, you'll get yours!

Okay, back to the women who need some good advice...I'm here for you. I have been there. Or maybe I'm still there. Some days are really good, some days aren't. You may be wondering how the heck you got into t his situation. Though you may be putting up a strong front for the world, you might be suffering inside trying to move on after divorce.

Whether your money is great or in short supply, whether you are happily dating or happily not dating, whether you know you are better off without him or you are pining for the man you planned on being with forever-you are not alone.

It always helps me to know that I'm not alone. That others have been through what I'm currently going through and lived to tell the tale. I had a heartfelt talk with my wonderful, classy, beautiful, smart mother about my divorce and berating myself for not being completely healed from it. She calmly let me know that I was not alone. Moms told me that it took her a long time to "officially" get over my dad after their divorce. Thankfully, they are on good terms, but for almost a decade they

18

weren't. I told my mom I felt like the pain of losing my best friend, my confidant, my ace boom boom was too much to bear and I would never move on after divorce. I'm going to sum up and give you the advice she gave to me:
You will have love again and not be scared to love back

- *One day you will wake up and know you have successfully moved on when you can wish him (and his new love) blessings and prosperity (instead of revenge and bad credit!)*
- *You are at peace with yourself, with him, and with the whole divorce mess.*
- *You can count it a blessing that your ex was once a part of your life and count your marriage and divorce as a valuable lesson in life.*
- *You no longer fantasize of calling your 2nd cousin *Pookie who knows a guy who knows a guy who could "teach that scumbag ex-husband of yours a good lesson, just say the word."*

*Okay, this last one isn't my classy mom's advice, but mine. Granted it still applies right?!

II. Taking responsibility - Your first step to healing

While at my father's place, swirling a glass of port, I asked him what helped him move on in his divorce from my mother. What he said surprised me, and helped me understand how he moved on so well from his wreckage of a marriage.

"The one thing that allowed me to heal more than any other was taking responsibility. Initially it was 50% of the responsibility, but after a time I realized the only way I could heal was to take on 100%. I had to completely embrace what I had done to damage the relationship rather than focus even an inkling on what your mother had done. It was very difficult and I embraced my many failings as a husband. This sounds negative but it was what allowed me to find peace and eventually forgive myself. After all, I think the only reason we wish to blame the other is so that we don't have to face ourselves." – Mike's Dad

Usually I am not surprised by what comes out of my father's mouth but this caught me off guard. I agree with this a MILLION percent! When you are able to take all the responsibility rather than a weak 50% you will find that you can finally move on. Forgive yourself and you will amazingly be able to forgive your ex. My father was absolutely right when he said we blame others to displace responsibility, don't do this; it is only prolonging your suffering.

I also completely agree with the wise words of Mike's father. Take responsibility woman! Until you take responsibility for your breakup and the mess you have made out of this relationship and others you will always be the passenger instead of the driver in the car of life. You will continue to be the ditch digger instead of the architect of your skyscraper that's your destiny. Worst of all…you will forever be the window shopper instead of the OWNER of those 6 inch hot pink open toed satin stilettos that other women (and fabulous gay men) are envious of!

Now you're probably saying, "But Mike and Kim, he cheated on me, wiped out our bank accounts, and kicked little dogs on numerous occasions! Why do I have to take responsibility for that?" And we will answer in unison, "Sweetie, you chose him." How do you think I became Kim Hess Divorce Guru? By taking responsibility and acknowledging that I chose this man to be my lover, my friend, the father of my children, my husband, and now my ex-husband.

I (wo)manned up and took responsibility that I allowed him to treat me like crap because I was scared to be on my own, and didn't have the cojones to stand up to him and demand to be treated as an equal. As soon as I took responsibility my life got better. Much better, much happier, which allowed me to forgive him and myself. I don't need any wounds on my heart…I'm way too cute for that!

Forgiveness and Surrender

This is a gift that you give yourself and him. The sooner one can do this, the sooner the pain will dissipate. I know it is hard but you must realize that if you were in his shoes you would have done the same thing.

21

Hell yeah I would've done the same thing! I would've partied at local clubs with hot single people while he stayed home with the kids and I would have partied in different countries with strippers while my loving partner cared for all the stuff going on at home. If I had been in his shoes I would have taken advantage just like he did...because **I let him.**

You must surrender to the fact that you cannot control the situation. You don't have your fingers on the mouse button of life directing where you want your surfing to go.

Let me add something...you can't control **other** people's situation either. You can only control you and yours. I couldn't control my ex's partying ways, but I could control how I reacted to them. I can't control how my ex lives his life now or how he reacts towards me, but I can control something far greater than my ex: **myself.** I've forgiven him and myself for our past, which has led me to surrender the pain I had in my heart and become a rock star!

I have run into a lot of divorced and single women out there, A LOT and although many of them have done a fantastic job of moving on, so many have not. Many women have never forgiven their ex for what he has done and have worked so hard at maintaining this emotional poison that it has become a part of them. This is something that you must avoid at all costs! (Yeah, and it gives you wrinkles and gray hair.)

"Holding onto anger is like drinking poison and expecting the other person to die." - Felice Dunas

I think most of us have heard this quote before, yet why do we not act on it? Why is it so sexy to hate our ex? It is almost as if it becomes a comfort to our soul to have someone to hate. As if it solidifies our place in life as the person that is in the RIGHT. The person that was injured, damaged, and wronged. (It doesn't. What it does is solidifies your place in life as a bitter woman.)

Supplemental Video: Anger and Projection
Lets explore this topic a little bit more. What does it mean for your future dating life to carry ANY anger into the next relationship.
http://www.startdatingagain.net/?page_id=68

III. Support and healing - Move past the pain

I don't have a ton of experience here so I will ask Kim to fill in the gaps.

Getting over anything as traumatic as a divorce or a bad breakup is too much for anyone to handle without help. Whether that help comes in the form of friends and family, a professional support group, online forum or professional counseling. Whatever method you choose you must find one because no one is an island and nothing heals more than to share and feel support from others that have suffered the same.

I cannot stress Mike's words enough. I would also like to encourage reaching out to others during hard times. We as women are usually the nurturers. We like to take care of loved ones, but when it comes time for us to be on the receiving end, we feel like we're not worthy. Going through the very rough times of my divorce I isolated myself and didn't reach out because I didn't want to "bother" anyone with my problems. I was more concerned with others supposed well-being over my own!

Let me ask you this. If you had a friend or family member who was in deep pain, an emotional mess, crying and rolled up into a ball in the corner of their bedroom floor who felt that no one in the world understood their pain, what would you do? You would want them to reach out to you! You would want them to pick up the phone and ask for help, right? You would also be relieved that they called you versus wallowing in their pain alone or doing something to harm themselves. So imagine how someone you love would react to you calling them up for a little empathy. Maybe they would have relief that you called? Provide a listening ear? Console you and maybe even make you laugh? Remember, Mike said no one is an island, and this is not the time to be stranded on one.

Dealing with the pain

Dealing with the pain of separation comes in two flavors: The first is wrapping yourself up in the pain and feeling the hurt. The other is looking the other way while time heals. I think that both of these are necessary in the healing process but it is very dependent upon who you are as to what you focus on. If you find you are the type of person to run from reality, diving in is the fastest way to healing. If you are the type to roll excessively in the pain of it all, you should be focusing more on allowing time to heal you.

Most of you will probably need to dive in first and struggle with the anaconda of your self-doubt. When this stage starts to become a little stagnant it is time to move on with your life and stop focusing on the pain.

Diving in

You're going to get a lot of advice on what to do and how to get through the pain of a devastating separation. Since I'm a Divorce Guru, I'm here to throw my two cents in. (which you will value like 2 million dollars...or that little black dress that makes you look 2 sizes smaller and your boobs 2 sizes bigger!)

Your first instinct will be the desire to get busy, distract yourself, to fill up your schedule and your life, to jump into your newly single status headfirst. Okay, sweetie, I gotcha, I feel your need to distract yourself from the pain. But first and foremost, I want you to sit down. Relax. Take a deep breath. And feel the pain.

You heard me right! I want you to feel the pain. Sit in it, bring it on, and roll around in it. Cry, yell, scream, stomp, and grab a pillow and punch, punch, punch. Why am I forcing you to surround yourself with this pain? So you can see it, immerse yourself in it, and come out the other end being a stronger better woman. Example time.

Remember having to swim a lap in gym class? What did we have to do first? Jump in. The water may have been cold, our hair was definitely getting messed up, and we had to get to the other side of the pool to pass gym and not have to repeat 10th grade. So we jumped in, got wet and swam. Then we got out, dried ourselves off and went to 5th period with that cute guy with the sexy eyes, knowing that we passed stupid gym class.

What happened to those girls who didn't jump in to the pool and swim to the other side? They didn't pass gym class. Which means they had to take it over and over and over, until they finally said "Aw, the hell with it", and did the stupid lap. Or they never did the lap, didn't pass that gym class, failed school altogether and didn't get to graduate. Which in the world of breakups and divorce means looking for the happy relationship that never happens. Or it could mean dying alone in an apartment with 70 cats all named Mr. Peepers and no one finding the body until the downstairs neighbors start to complain about the smell. Equally great scenarios, take your pick.

Do you want this to be you? Didn't think so. Dive in, get wet, and get healed. I promise you, you'll come out on the other side a better person because of it. Trust me.

26

Now that you've jumped into the "pool" and successfully completed your laps, we can talk about distraction.

Distraction Distraction Distraction

I don't know where I read it but one of the treatments used for PTSD (post traumatic stress disorder) for Vietnam vets was to keep them occupied. Simply put they would put these guys to work and force their focus away from past pains they have suffered. This is an excellent way to distract the mind so that it won't dwell upon a painful place. There is no reason why you can't do the same thing.

I don't want to go to work!

So many times I have wanted to go to work as much as I wanted to put hot sauce on my genitals. (Don't lie, you can relate). However, amazingly while at work, your focus changed, you snapped out of your miserable mood and felt great by the end of your shift. If you never had gone to work you would have wallowed in your misery the entire day.

Changing your focus is what moves you to the next stage of healing. You are transitioning from wallowing in your pain to taking control back. It is time to turn you back on the thoughts that will drag you back down into mascara blackened misery.

When my pet of 18 years took her last breath in my arms, I was destroyed. I had been training for the Nagano Marathon only three weeks away. My training partner understood and gave me a week to mourn but I am incredibly thankful that after a week she pulled me back to reality. "Mike, I know you are still hurting and the last thing you want to do is train, but it is time." She was right, I really really really didn't want to train but it was time and the training helped me take the next step. My grieving was finished but it took a close friend's firmness to have me see that.

When you are ready, let's kill the negative focus until that filthy corner of pain fades from lack of attention.

Changing your focus:

* Get in shape, change the diet and start to work out daily
* Put in more hours at work (not so healthy but works)
* Volunteer with homeless, special needs children
* Change your career (do what you have always dreamed)
* Go back to school
* Girl's night out (no one to go with? Fucking find them!!!)
* Go on a rebound?
* Start a business!
* Travel... ahhhhh...my personal love! (Be crazy and spend 6 months on the Peace Boat!! Or how about a working holiday in Australia? Go to Brazil and study dance? I will never forget the three months I spent doing nothing in Thailand)

Remove all reminders

If you have kids this is a rough one but still possible. Clearly you don't want to isolate your children from any reminders of their father but you can still make an impact. (Have your kids put daddy's picture in their room, or better yet a family photo album that they can keep in their room to have access to.)

28

To my surprise I have had friends get out of a relationship and still leave tons of reminders around. I'm not talking about the microwave the two of you bought together on sale, but fricken' pictures in the bedroom of the two of you. In the bedroom? Really? Not only is this not good for moving on but it is incredibly off putting for any new man that might visit!

Is this you? Do you have pictures of your ex all around your home? Still have some of his clothes? Get rid of them. You need that space freed up for the better things in life. Take his picture out of the frame and replace it with one of you in your sexiest outfit or having fun! Getting his clothes out of your closet may mean more room for your clothes…or the clothes of the new sexy man who will one day be in your life!

Look around your home and take stock of all the things that are halting your healing and put them in a damn box! Want a zit to heal? Stop picking at it! All the emotional landmines around your home may not be helping you. Maybe you even need to go as far as to move?

Do yourself a favor though; don't throw everything away, once you pass through the healing mine field, you might want to savor again some of the warm memories you once shared.

I agree Mike, even if it takes 50 years to heal and be able to look at the pictures, I'm assuming you had some good times at least once…plus the kids always get a kick out of what mommy looked like with big hair and shoulder pads!

Moving on Bullets:

- Before you can move on are you truly ready? A rebound relationship is only a Band-Aid over what might need stitches.
- There are no divorce police! Which means your morality is your guide, not your neighbors, not your mothers.
- Diving into your pain is the fastest way to move away from it, don't be afraid it won't kill you.
- Once you are done mourning, STOP IT! many people don't finish this process and it progresses into angry bitterness. When you are finished, distract yourself to move away from the potentially addictive thinking pattern.
- Taking 100% responsibility is the first step to forgiveness and peace. Most anger is generated from a need to be right, but this is drinking ones own poison.
- Changing your focus or "spotlighting" is a flashlight in the dark room of your subconscious. Guide it by removing all painful reminders, create lists of affirmation, get inspirational emails, and stop watching divorce court!

Actions:

Moving on from the ex is only passive in the sense that time heals but I am sure you would like to speed up this process as much as possible! To do so we need to act, not just ruminate over the previous chapters.

1. Find a support group in your area, write down the place/time and stick it to your fridge!
2. Take inventory of your home/apartment/computer what needs to go!?? Now call a girlfriend, get some wine and start cleaning!

3. Are you using the valuable recourses of your friends and family? If not get on the phone now and ask for the support you need, I assure you they will give it to you.
4. If you find taking 100% responsibility hard it is time to take steps to understand this concept. Make a list of how and why you were responsible for what occurred in your relationship. Even physical violence you can be responsible for, if you didn't see that as a signal to leave instantly.
5. If you find taking 100% responsibility hard it is time to take steps to understand this concept. Make a list of how and why you were responsible for what occurred in your relationship. Even physical violence you can be responsible for, if you didn't see that as a signal to leave instantly.
6. Do you need more help here? No one can take the next step into a healthy relationship without being healed. Maybe you need to seek professional help first? If you don't heal, forgive, and understand, you are bound to repeat it.

Part two: Preparation

I am assuming that you have the move-on part covered and you are ready to get out there and DATE! Well, before you do that lets have a little bit of fun. Before we go out on the town we need to figure out who we want to choose! Right? But, how can we hit a target that we have not even drawn? In the process of helping finding that target Kim and I are going to make fun a bit of the typical morons you are going to run into and help you avoid them. At the same time we want to present some of the winners that might be eluding you.

Of course the point is to find the perfect guy and this takes a combination of knowing what you want and repelling what you don't want. Since so many of us are drawn to people that support our dysfunctions, we want to aggressively steer you away from them. The last thing we/you want is for you to boomerang back to your ex or someone just like him.

Finally I would like you to understand the game, how all this attraction stuff works. Don't think you need this? I would argue it is what you need the most, very few people understand attraction or why they keep screwing it up. I want to not only teach you the typical pitfalls women go through but I want to arm you with the tools and knowledge necessary to get him and keep him. It isn't that complicated but by understanding just a little bit of what is going on under the surface you leap forward in his estimation of you.

IV. The who - Who stinks, who doesn't

The Bad, the good, and the stupid

Okay lest have a little bit of fun! Who are the idiots you are going to run into along the way to the perfect guy.

Mr. Master Dater and I have each made up a handy dandy list of the men who are bound to come into your newly single life. We want to save you a lot of time and heartache by cluing you in on avoiding the bad guys and speed your way towards someone worthy of your time!

Mike's list signs and men you need to avoid!

1. **Commit o' Phobe** - Never been married and considers a long relationship 1 year -Well this discredits me immediately! This reminds me of what my friend Jack says, "Him being married before means that he has a stamp on his commitment card," excellent point, and one that really matters.

2. **The Horn Dog** - Is he hinting at you riding the baloney pony your first meeting? Crap... not a good sign, most likely he is there for sex, not relationship. Unless he has some sort of sexual tourettes I would move on right away, OR do what my friend Shannon does and sleep with him anyway!

3. **Dopey** - Hey, who doesn't smoke a little pot these days (except me, can't stand the stuff), or have a cocktail periodically. If that is the case then go for it but if he offers you "some of the good stuff" on the first date he might have a problem. People with addictive personalities don't make very good partners, unless of course you need someone to bring your own addictions to new heights!

4. **Mr. Prick** - Ahh... the sexy asshole that you keep justifying to friends and family that, "You just don't know what he is like when we are alone." Sigh... I thought you might be grown up by now? Are you still susceptible to the guy that feeds your insecurities?? Come on girl! Join a support group and get the fuck over it!

5. **The Workaholic** - This guy seems really attractive initially because he is so industrious. How can someone not respect a guy that puts in 16 hour days, 6 days a week? First, people don't change, you know that. Now... ask yourself, where do I fit into that kind of work week? Do I do him during his coffee breaks? Or while he is sleeping?

6. **Money Bags, or The Hobo** - He makes significantly less/more $ than you. This kind of imbalance will only lead to insecurities on one side or the other. But he is mega rich!? Unless he is willing to split his income with you 50/50 you will become his property, no exceptions. He is ultra poor? Do you really want to carry his loser ass for the next five years while he drinks beer and complains about the economy?

7. **Mr. Rim Chew** - The nice guy is surprisingly just as bad as the asshole with a couple of major differences.

You respect the asshole and/or might actually be able to have an orgasm with him. The nice guy? Probably neither, sure the lack of tension feels nice but without that tension where is the attraction? To really be happy you need to have that tension, minus the asshole part. A lot of people don't realize that positive tension is a wondrous attribute in a relationship. Negative tension or no tension is the doom of any relationship.

8. **HunkaSaurus** – He is way hotter than you. If you have even an inkling of feeling like this the relationship might be doomed. It isn't because he is so sexy that he is going to leave you, it is because you feel insecure enough to sabotage the relationship! So just assume that he is gay and move on to someone you feel more comfortable with. Does this mean you date someone you don't find so attractive?? NO!!! just as dangerous, never settle, ever... I can't stress enough how dangerous "good" is, it is the number one thing that is blocking you from finding "GREAT!"

9. **Two Pump Chump** - A friend of mine is married to a really really good looking guy. Once when talking to her it came out, "Bob is so handsome but is so bad in bed I want to cry. He apologizes for only being able to stay erect for 2 minutes but it is so frustrating!" Any guy that doesn't do his DAMNEDST to fix this, for the woman he loves, isn't worth staying with. This is a selfish move and it pains me deeply that this part of her relationship is seriously lacking. Slap some fucking Viagra in his hand, or point him to the door.

10. **Captain Awesome** – This guy loves pumping every story up and one-upping not only his friends but you! His ego is so weak that he will waste no opportunity to put you down to boost him and his little penis up. Find

yourself in a relationship with one of these morons? I would suggest backing out of that relationship cautiously, since he will be more than happy to build a fantastic story about how you destroyed everything.

11. **Sarge!** - This person obviously doesn't have to be a military guy, but we often see it from this type of career. This guy found that he was the greatest, healthiest and happiest when someone was pulling his strings and now thinks that everyone, including his kids needs to be micromanaged into misery. There is no changing this kind of guy, until he gets cancer and on his deathbed finally apologizes for being an asshole.

12. **Bromancing the Stone** - The dude with too many buddies is very similar to the workaholic. His life revolves around his friends not around you. He could be and probably is, the coolest guy ever but if asked: buddies or relationship? Will always choose buddies. This type of guy is in eternal bromances and probably will never be able to give you the time you need.

13. **David Koresh** - Was it the Kool-aid? Strangely enough this guy will put up with your atheist ass in order to get a little ass, but as soon as things get a little serious the pressure is on! If you don't instantly stop drinking coffee and start wearing the correct underwear you will be 86-ed like I was, at 3 in the morning, at Denny's last Saturday.

14. **Double Take** – He is your twin! This is a sneaky one that you may not expect, he seems cool, you have a lot in common, and initially a lot to talk about. Why is this a problem? Well because the second you stop having things in common to talk about is the second you will be bored out of your mind. People that are

interesting are the ones that create excitement in our lives, and inevitably those people are the ones that are very very different than we are. The kind of guy you are looking for is someone that can positively expand who you are as a person. How in the world could someone with all the same beliefs and views make you a more rounded person?

15. **The Lazy Boy** - This is the guy that was really upset when the A-team finally got canceled. He hates anything new and as a result will be very hard to grow with, only choose this kind of guy if you are reckless and need someone to rein you in, but I imagine you would want to kill him after a week. Just make sure you hide the body well.

Kim's Bad Boys

1. Permanent Bachelor - I've dated several men who have no kids, never been married and it was tough. You might have fun, but as long term goes, you two probably don't view life the same. And what happens if you one day WANT commitment? He's going to run away screaming no commitment, no commitment! Why? Because he's used to his bachelorhood and set in his ways.

If he's never been in a long term, committed relationship do you really want to be the one to break him in? That guy who's never been married, engaged, cohabitated or even dated anyone for longer than 3 months. At 35? 45? or 55? He's set in his ways, maybe a tad selfish and now that I think about it, why has he never made a commitment? I've had women say to me: "Well, what about George Clooney, he's a great catch"? I can almost guarantee this guy ain't George Clooney, and little known fact, George Clooney is divorced. Meaning he was once committed. The guy I'm talking about…not even close.

37

2. Too Soon Too Fast - Ladies, I've learned the hard way that men tell you what they want quickly. If he says he's looking for marriage, believe him (this probably means marriage with any willing woman, not just you 'cause you're special.) If he says he doesn't want a relationship, believe him. If he talks about sex during the first email, phone call or date he just wants sex. He's told you what he wants. Believe him. Not a girlfriend, not a friend, but sex.

If he, as Mike would say, starts talking about riding the baloney pony over your first dinner...well, that's what he wants-and that's all he wants. He tries to stick his tongue down your throat after the first date? Well, consider that just an appetizer to what he wants for dessert! Don't kid yourself that if you give up the goods that he will then want a relationship.

3. Already Committed - I know, I know, his girlfriend just doesn't get him. His wife is mean to him, but he's staying for the kids. Or the dogs. Or the parakeets. Or he can't afford to leave. There are a multitude of reasons. Whatever it is, the guy is married and you will be way down on his list of priorities. The fact is you are less than, even disposable or replaceable. You're the "chick on the side". You are not one of his top priorities. You deserve more, so be with a man who is available to give you more. I've had this guy. The heartache ain't worth it when he will never be truly available to you anyway.

4. Smokes pot all day everyday - Picture this: first date with this super cute, tall, intellectual, beautiful blue-eyed man. We met for drinks, he took me to an expensive restaurant, and held my hand as we walked down the moonlit sidewalk. Make a romantic long story short, we went back to my place where he blazed up a blunt. As I passed on his kind offer to "take a toke" I just assumed this was an every now and then thing to him. After many months of dating, I find out he smokes weed every day. Everyday! Sometimes 2, 3 times a day! If someone's life

38

choices do not reflect your own it is going to sicken you every time he blazes up, I don't care how hot he is.

5. The Jerk - He's mean to waitresses! He sneers at small children. He doesn't hold the door open for little old ladies. This is the jerk who is rude to people, arrogant, and narcissistic. I've dated this guy. I married this guy. What was my excuse? "I know he's kind of a jerk, but he's nice to me!" But let me tell you, if he's a jerk to everyone else, he's going to end up being a jerk to you. Probably more so, because you have to deal with him more and he knows you will put up with it. Can I reiterate how much you should take this advice?

6. Cheapskate - Quibbles over a dollar tip, yeah you heard me. I was on a second date with a guy, an actor. We split a cheap lunch...12 bucks total. He made me pay ½. Strike one. I gave him my half plus tip and he put down $15 dollars for the tab-I assumed 12 dollars for the bill and a $3 tip. He asked the waitress for a dollar back. A dollar! Would it have killed him to leave her a $3 tip? You might rationalize that because he is male and you are really really lonely that somehow this is acceptable. The reality is that money fights are the number one couple killer and if you are disgusted with his money attitude now you are going to HATE it later.

7. Mr. Pig - He's a chauvinist...as in believes women are the inferior race. He'll make comments about how his boss only got the job because she has big boobs. He'll reiterate how his mom never complained and always had a fresh martini and hot dinner waiting for his father every day. When he's on the road he'll state that women shouldn't be allowed to drive. Yeah, chuckle it up with him sister...until you realize he actually thinks he's better than you because he's a man. Oh yeah, that's respect for you.

8. It's all about him - Does he only want to please himself? Is he kind and considerate towards you? A man who doesn't

39

want to please his partner is not a real man. This pertains to outside of the bedroom a well as in. Example: he wants to meet for your first date in HIS city or neighborhood, in the winter, in a snowstorm. Doesn't he know you're going to be wearing heels and a tight skirt? He doesn't believe you're worth the trip to your neck of the woods? Evidently not. Dump him, and dump him now, if he's not interested in coming to you, he probably not interested in making you cum.

9. Talks about Ex…All the time - Beware the man who speaks of his ex-wife or ex-girlfriend on a regular basis to you. If the man you're interested in is constantly talking about another woman…let him go. Whether he's talking about how much he misses her or how much he hates her it means he's thinking about her and not you. He's still hung up on her and needs to get over his longing for her…without your help.

10. Mama's Boy - True story. I met a 35-year-old man that took his mother to shop for clothes with him. Maybe he has horrible taste but she even went into the dressing room with him! Remember, this is a true story! If you want this man in your life you gotta realize that your life will be controlled by her as well. Run, fast before his mama is choosing your wedding dress and deciding where you spend your vacations.

I imagine a lot of these guys sound familiar to you. Why is that? Because you have dated them, avoided them, and fallen in love with them. Sure most of them are easy to ID but what about the ones that you keep seeming to date!!?? What is up with that? Why do you keep repeating the same mistakes? If so read the article below to finally stop this cycle.

Using what you can't you stand about that A**hole!
By Mike Masters

The necessity of mistakes

Whenever we learn a new task we do so by making mistakes. We keep the goal in mind and bounce off of mistake after mistake until we learn. The problem is that many people do not recognize their mistakes and continue to repeat them. This is like burning your fingers on the stove over and over again, never associating flame with pain. (Or like my cousin who uses abortion as a form of birth control)

My biggest relationship error

I used to be madly in love/hate with Keiko, when it was good it was great and when it was bad it was a nightmare. When things were bad we would fight and threaten to cut things off (the relationship, and/or body parts) but very soon we would both look the other way, basking in the illusion of a wonderful relationship. Sound familiar?

When you focus on one thing or another you are doing something called spotlighting. I was heavily spotlighting with Keiko. I was only looking at the good and ignoring the bad. After our 6th, yes 6th break up I decided I was finished! I needed to stop forgetting why I was so unhappy the second we got naked. I needed to turn my mental spotlight on the negative and stop ignoring what was so obvious to everyone but myself.

In a fervor I wrote three long lists of why I needed to leave Keiko. I took these lists, recorded them and put them on my iPod. I would listen to these lists once in the morning and every time I started to think about the good times with "sweet" Keiko. "NO!!" I would yell at myself and quickly listen to my iPod, nodding, "That's right... I forgot about that." This change of focus helped me pry myself away from this super unhealthy relationship. Want to hear my list?
http://www.mikethemasterdater.com/wp-content/uploads/2009/03/spotlight-break-up-example.mp3

Have you ever noticed that you have more drive to lose weight than to be healthier? That it is easier to move away from pain than it is to move towards pleasure? This is a part of human nature that is not necessarily negative and is something we can use pry bar to get us away from what

41

does us true damage. Focusing on the negative, building it, in order to avoid it can be very positive.

How to never date THAT kind of guy again

Think of every frustrating, obnoxious, annoying, childish, selfish thing he did and get a little pissed off. Now get a little more pissed off and write down what you hate!

What things will I never again tolerate?

1. A smoker
2. A man that is more concerned with TV than me
3. Someone that thinks 5 minutes of sex is acceptable
4. A guy that doesn't fucking SNORE
5. Someone with a loving family that can accept my religious views
6. A man that removes his stress with two bottles of wine
7. I am disgusted by cheaters and I will never again accept infidelity
8. Dishonesty of any kind I cannot accept
9 – 20

This is your new fuel towards a healthier relationship. You have now defined the painful hot stove you need to forever avoid. Spending time and really turning up the volume of this pain will help you never again repeat it. I suggest putting this list somewhere you can reference it in a time of need. I also suggest reviewing it daily until you feel it had forever bound with the weak neurons that are attracted to this kind of ass. Good Hunting.

Good guy signs

Now we've warned you about the guys to run from, avoid, and not speak to even if your life depended on it. Now to the good guys, who will make your life pleasant, drama free, and lemony fresh. Okay maybe not lemony-fresh but happy!

Mike's Good Guys…

1. **He is open to sharing the bad** - He doesn't appear to keep any secrets, he is willing to tell you things that might make a lesser man uncomfortable. A man like this has learned that complete self-acceptance means your "flaws" define you, which is not necessarily a bad thing. The limit to this is if he starts telling sex stories about when he was in Thailand for a month.

2. **Is still "friends" with his ex (but not too much)** - He is mature and adult enough to be able to reconcile his differences with his ex. He sees himself as separate from her and thus is able to forgive her and himself. The immature man has his self-worth tied up in her rejection of him, and needs to reject her in turn. Although this can be dangerous, since if there is still that "connection" you might not be the only one interested in having his baby.

3. **Has kids and is a good father** - Great! I like to think most guys are like this, but it certainly is not the standard. This not only shows quality of character but a level of commitment to others beyond himself. In converse, I know a guy that has three kids in two countries and doesn't give a rat's ass about any of them. If you want his number I would be happy to offer it.

4. **Is passionate but not angry** - Passion and anger is often a mixed trait, you want a guy that is passionate about his life and dreams but not angry! Since it is often hard to differentiate passion from aggression, some businesses conduct interviews during a game of golf, and nothing brings out emotional outburst more than a nice slice. If you don't happen to have a golf course

handy, make him sit through "The English Patient" and if he doesn't punch something you might want to bet on this horse.

5. **Horny, but under control** - I like this, I really respect the person that is highly sexual but classy enough to STFU when it is inappropriate. I probably respect this because I am NOT one of these people.

6. **Respectful enough not to look at the waitresses ass** - This hangs out with the one above, any guy that is out with you but can not control his eyes is a sorry excuse for a man. With that said... If you ever go out with me, try to look the other way or I will wear sunglasses, whichever you prefer.

7. **Is Open to communication** - Okay duh... Yeah I know you know this, but you might be in a bit of a crush/in-love situation and may be ignoring the fact that it seems to always be his way or the highway. Also understand the opposite; don't mistake good communication for him being like Dudley Doright, trying to meet your every need. Good communication is someone that not only is willing to listen but to truly "hear" your meaning. Don't you just hate those people that don't listen and are only waiting to talk!? Now, what did you say again?

8. **Doesn't put up with your bullshit** - This one is a really big deal, you know when you are being a shit to him and he says, "you are being a shit, cut it out." Doesn't that kick ass??? A guy that has the meat sac to stand up to you is someone that you can respect and stay with. If he can't do this? Well, just walk on him and make him pay for everything, after all that is probably what he wanted in the first place.

9. **Doesn't get jealous, except when appropriate** - This one took me a long time to figure out. I was either horribly jealous or didn't care at all. I think it is very important for him to be confident enough not to freak out over you having 26 ex-boyfriends on your Facebook. However, I also think it is important for him to show he actually gives a shit when you go to the "Thunder Down Under" male strip show in Vegas, he may not even care but at least he has the wits to fake it well enough so you feel cared about.

10. **Is different from you, expands your life** - Being with someone different is crucial to growth because all of us need to push the boundaries of our innermost fears. Maybe, you are killer at numbers and always get your taxes in months before they're due, maybe he is a artist that hasn't filed taxes in 10 years. This is a good match, you may need to relax your sphincter a bit, and he needs to stop hugging so many trees.

11. **Able to grow with you** - The ultimate gift is being with someone that is moving at the same speed you are. It doesn't have to be in the same direction necessarily, but there has to be growth. If one partner is stagnant and you are reaching for the stars there will inevitably be a time when you will grow so much, that one of you will be sabotage the relationship out of intimidation/frustration. Relationship balance is something we can control if aware of, although there is a limit and this is why income gaps, career gaps and attraction gaps, are potentially so dangerous. Don't marry a gardener if you aspire to be a doctor.

12. **Substance use is limited or not used** - Hey, I love a glass of wine every once in a while. I also like a girl

that can have a couple of beers and know when to stop. Alcohol is a wonderful social lubricant, and used in the right quantities can be a whole lot of fun. Any man/woman that is out of college and STILL likes to get slobbering drunk is on their way to a much larger problem. I have to admit I am horribly drawn to someone that brings out this demon in me and if they are hot, I am DOOMED.

13. **Likes to exercise** - Maybe you don't exercise and if that is the case, damn it! You should!! Guys and girls that work out regularly are radically different than people that don't. Sex is better, life is better, fuck... everything is better! Please understand I don't mean a guy in his thirties that is obsessed with his body (Me..). This... not a good sign, he should have gotten over the fact that girls didn't like him in High School a LONG time ago. Not a winner and probably a cheater, driven to satisfy insecurities of the past.

14. **Works to live not lives to work (unless it is his passion)** - There is a fine line between someone that is a workaholic or has passion for their work. A workaholic is someone that works for works sake, the same reason an alcoholic drinks. It is a way to escape life, as long as they are "busy" or "drunk" life can't "get them." Someone with a passion for their work is someone you want to be around, someone that can inspire you! However, he needs to have self control over his passion and not have his love life crash into tree, because like me, he is working 16 hours a day, 7 days a week. Hell, I am blinking blood from looking at this damn screen so long.

15. **Accepts you the way you are** - This is super duper important, he doesn't like the way you look?

Doesn't like your job? Your clothes, Sister, or dog? Big problem, which will probably be reconciled by you picking him apart as well. Unfortunately, a lot of men and women will be fully accepting of their partner when they are in a good space themselves. The second they feel uncomfortable with their own life situation they will project this frustration upon you in a displacement maneuver. This is when you maneuver them over to a mirror and force them to take a good long look...

Kim's Good Guy...

This is pretty easy for me and I don't think I need any descriptions. Mike's list was funny but I am going to be down to earth and keep it simple sister! Hopefully my definition of a fantastic guy will resonate with you too.

1. Values spirituality in his life
2. He can tie his own shoes
3. A skateboard isn't his major mode of transportation (don't laugh, I've met men in their late 30's who only get around town on a skateboard!)
4. Someone who believes weed is a recreational drug and not to be used everyday like a multivitamin.
5. Ambitious
6. Realizes that if I have to shave my legs, he has to shave his back
7. Believes that men paying for a first date is just a nice thing to do.
8. Holds doors open for old ladies.
9. Holds doors open for me.
10. Brings me tea/breakfast in bed.
11. Enjoys life instead of complaining about it.
12. Tells me I look pretty.
13. Asks me if I've lost weight.

14. Won't drool over the 21 year old bouncing around the beach in the string bikini THEN suggest I go on a diet.
15. Offers (not demands) to order for me at his favorite restaurant.
16. Walks me home, in the rain.
17. Walks street side.
18. Asks me how my day went.
19. Asks me how my kids are doing.
20. Says, "Wow, I can't believe you had two kids!"
21. Holds my hand.
22. Let's an old man have his seat on the subway.
23. Speaks highly of his mom, the mother of his children if he has any, and women in general.
24. Tells me how beautiful I am, inside and out.
25. Respects me and tells me so.
26. Works at keeping up not only his appearance, but also expanding his mind

Hopefully we have given you ideas as to what to look for, or avoid in a man. Many of these you already knew and we want to reinforce that knowledge!

I want to take this a step further though and really look deeply into who really is perfect for you and why. Most people have no idea who they are attracted to and why, they say one thing, "I want someone who is a kind, understanding, and honest person" then they date the complete opposite. This is for two reasons, one is because the subconscious mind is making the choice not the conscious and the SC chooses men that reinforce it's perception of who you are and what you deserve. (I will get into more detail in a later chapter) The second reason is because men and women don't understand the "type" of person that is really good for them. Rather they are driven by attraction only, not an educated choice.

So first lets figure out who is your perfect partner and why.

V. Understanding who you are and who your perfect partner is

Do you see the chart above? Somewhere on that chart is where your personality is dominant and somewhere is your opposite, the person that will be perfect in your life.

I wrote about this concept long before I discovered a book that laid out everything completely. I credit Dr. Paul for putting this information together for me to understand and to pass it on to you. To learn more go to his website at http://www.kwml.com Dr. Paul's work is based on Carl Jung's work on the human archetypes, Dr. Paul just took it one step further and in a stroke of brilliance related it to relationships. Pay attention to this section, it is remarkably true and you have probably never heard it before.

The first split - the masculine and the feminine

For years I had been confused why so many people assumed I was gay. For a long time this was very frustrating but eventually I just accepted it and became comfortable in my own shoes. Only much later did I understand why people assumed this of me and why I found myself so attracted to assertive, wild, slightly selfish women. It was because I had "feminine" attributes, I was a nurturer, patient, passive, and emotional. Did this make me gay? Of course not, but I did find myself attracted to my "masculine" female counter part.

First lets understand the masculine/feminine divide in the diagram below.

This separation is pretty strait forward, and if masculine and feminine energy offends you, just use fire and water. So which side of the coin are you?

Feminine/Water – just like water, feminine energy absorbs, it is stable and constant, the feminine nurtures and is most satisfied in a giving position. They are comfortable seeing what happens, flowing into every situation.

The feminine character often has problems with people "walking" on them and "taking advantage" this is why the feminine characteristic is often the victim.

Masculine/Fire – just like fire, masculine energy consumes, it is unstable and assertive, masculine people are aggressive, they are not patient, they are takers and insist on their position in life/relationships.

The Masculine has a problem with getting into trouble because they are always "right", they don't like to back down and often unwittingly trample the feminine.

Okay, Master dater I understand that I am more on the feminine side but what about the girls that find themselves on the masculine? I am sure that no woman wants to be a Wo-Man! How can they be comfortable knowing that they carry masculine qualities?

Good question and is the most common resistance I get from this classification. One must think of this as energy only and not get hung up on cultural opinions of what is male or female. Having masculine traits does not make you a man; you are still very much a woman with feminine needs. This classification is only to help you understand who you are and who you should be dating.

For example very fiery women will fit with two types of partners, a passive feminine guy or, a really assertive, highly masculine guy. The assertive highly masculine guy, needs to out "man" you in order to have attraction. Unfortunately, attraction does not discern between healthy and unhealthy and this highly assertive guy will often be dysfunctionally masculine and you will be uncomfortable being pushed out of the space you are usually occupying.

In the above example John is super masculine and he is forcing Shannon to the feminine but this will never make her comfortable since she is not feminine. There might be a ton of tension here, and thus great sex but it is not healthy tension since Shannon is not in her natural fiery position.

The second split – the creative and logical

The split of the Creative and the Logical is something that I was not aware of until I read Dr. Paul's work, it was the missing puzzle piece for me and added to my understanding of relationship balance.

This split I think is much easier to understand and accept than the previous split but it is no less important.

Logical/Analytical – this type is very cut and dry, black and white. There are no shades of grey, in this person's life. They are as logical as Mr. Spock, and if masculine often emotionless. The logical person organizes their sock drawer, plans vacations, saves money, and is not comfortable with the unknown.

Creative/lackadaisical – this person is not constrained by the limits of culture and society. They find joy in the unknown, and associate pain with confinement. They are often messy, seeing order as a hindrance to more important creative pursuits. This person pays for the plane ticket the night before, doesn't book a hotel room, and probably doesn't bring enough money. They are more prone to having a wonderful adventure or a complete nightmare.

I am certainly the later, although I have learned to be more logical in order to avoid disaster. I have many times dated the logical type of girl and I have to admit it is great, they pickup where I falloff and there is a lot of harmony here. I also find that I have created a lot of great friendships with more analytical people.

My stepfather and my mother were both highly creative but he was very masculine and she feminine, so there was balance. However, there was no balance in the creative department and I remember them competing while I was growing up. After my mother's artwork was accepted into the Smithsonian my stepfather's resentment was palatable. Having friends, or lovers that take up the same region of your character often stifles our growth and joy in the relationship.

The Archetypes

Let's put it all together and give names to the four quadrants of human character.

So what am I? I am feminine and creative, that makes me a lover. Am I really a lover? Yes but so much more, we all have many of the qualities of the archetypes, so don't let this hinder your thinking, rather see it as a guide. Who is the character I am most suited for? Well, let me ask you this, would I have much to offer a partner identical to myself? The answer is no, we are most intrigued and attracted to people different than ourselves. So yes the cheesy Paula Abdul song "Opposites Attract" was correct, but Scat Cat was still stupid.

Mike, I did my chart and I am also "Feminine" and "Creative" which I'm guessing is why we get along so well! But, would you tell me this is why we've maintained a long and trouble free relationship as friends? If we were romantically involved does us being the same "type" spell disaster? Do I steer clear of my "next" being the same type?

This is an excellent question, yes Kim and I cover the same area, but we share equal interests, and also because we are both passive we are very polite to one another. Why else? Because, I am Kim's relationship coach, she asks questions constantly, we have a teacher student dynamic. Does this put me over her? No of course not, but... once Kim has learned what she can from me, will she be driven to call me, email me?? Probably not. Now, you must understand that I love Kim, she is awesome, she is so sweet and cool, could I date her? Maybe, for a little while, but we would both find the attraction difficult to maintain because the Tug O' War rope of sexual tension is too short and therefore not as much fun.

Should Kim steer clear of someone like herself romantically? YES!!!! That is the entire point of this chapter!! Sure people are more complicated than the above chart, and you probably could make a go of things, however, there is undoubtedly more attraction to someone different than you, than someone the same.

The Danger of a Teacher/Student relationship

Kim and I have a ton of respect for one another so we wouldn't fall into this trap as friends, but there is a huge danger here. Everyone has the desire to contribute and everyone has the desire to learn, but if that is all your relationship is based on, what happens when the student is finished or the teacher has nothing to teach? What holds a teacher student relationship together is a gap of power, the teacher giving and the student receiving, but here is an imbalance and in a sexual

57

relationship it is very very unhealthy. People need to be equals for relationship health to be maintained; otherwise one person ends up the slave and the other the master.

What Archetype are you?

Here is a more detailed explanation of the archetypes. Don't be held back by the male terminology.

The King/Queen - Nurturing, passive, logical and orderly, likes to direct things and issue commands, they are natural leaders. Characterized by wisdom, others often come to them for advice.

The Warrior - Confident and active, ready to dive into the activity that needs to be done. Logical and orderly like the King/Queen. The Warrior is a force of defense and protection of friends and family, a force of industriousness and ambition. These are the go-to people for when there is a task to be done.

The Magician - Full of emotional confidence, like the Warrior, but is very creative, adventurous, and so capable, that others might see their actions as magic. These people are performers, salespeople, and are "naturals" at making things happen. They dream big, get big results and are the center of celebration and attention.

The Lover - Artistic and creative like the Magician, but nurturing and passive like the King/Queen. These are the storytellers of society, and the shy musicians and writers, they are the romantics, the poets, the loving nurturers of society, and the fools who make us laugh and cry.

So your opposite is really your perfect match, why is this? The reason is surprisingly simple; we all wish to have all the qualities of all the archetypes. In other words, we wish to be the most rounded person possible, able to overcome the weaknesses of the archetype we were born into. Your opposite is the person that pulls you in the direction of your weakness and vice versa.

A long time ago I met someone that was my exact opposite and I fell in love. She was a radio DJ and an amazing powerful Warrior! This is what our relationship looked like

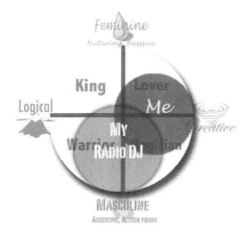

We over lapped a little bit but it is nearly impossible not to, this was the closest match I had ever found. Interestingly, if you take your closest friends, I mean BEST friends ever, and plot the two of you on a chart, you will find a similar balance.

Our relationship was initially amazing but soon utterly failed because the two other essential components necessary for all relationships to succeed were missing.

Those two components are Power Balance and Sexual
Tension.

VI. A quick guide to Power balance and Sexual tension

So why did the above relationship spontaneously combust like the Hindenburg? Well the first thing was that the Power balance was screwed up, she was making a few hundred thousand a year and I had a teacher's salary. Second, we just didn't have any sexual tension in the relationship, she was too young and inexperienced and everything was awkward. We probably would have been much better friends than lovers but because we were nearly a perfect archetype balance we were irresistibly drawn to each other. If I had known then what I know now I would have never entered that situation, although I would have been tempted.

The below tools of sexual tension and power balance will not only help you choose the right person but it will help you maintain the relationship if you are vigilant.

Before you move on to the next section it would be very helpful to watch this video in order to understand this crucial and difficult concept. Join Kim and I as we explore this.
Video: Sexual Tension
http://www.startdatingagain.net/?page_id=54

Sexual Tension

All attraction can be boiled down to one simple concept, tension. Humans and animals are programmed to seek out the highest quality mate that they can, in order to have the highest quality offspring. How do they gauge this? Tension.

Humans and animals constantly push the boundaries of what is acceptable, to test that tension in a potential mate. This is why one must accept and escalate the tension being created by the other person as well as create your own.

Earlier I explained that the reason you are so attracted to your opposite is because we all of the desire to learn, to grow, to become a whole complete person. This is why some of the most beautiful sexual tension is based on the respect and desire to learn the power our partner possesses. Once again this is why are closest friends are often so different than us. They ignite the tension of growth, the excitement of the unknown we wish to understand and become.

While knowing that your opposite is the person who carries that tension is one step in the understanding but it does not encompass the concept of tension. Sexual tension has many facets and even two people with similar qualities can experience this tension.

Let's say for example there is a very handsome manager at your work, he is older, very bright and unapologetic. One day, after a friend's drunken birthday, you turn in a report that is substandard. You are pulled into his office and kindly reprimanded, you are angry at him and yourself, but you are disturbed by how much you think of him. In fact you actually find yourself fantasizing about him inappropriately and from that point on you secretly seek his approval in the work place. Even though you mildly tell yourself you hate him, this hate is just as intense as the attraction.

To your discomfort and excitement, you find yourself alone with him at a business convention. You are surly with him but after a couple of drinks he breaks you down and you go to his room and the two of you screw like bunnies on ecstasy. It is one of the best sexual/emotional experiences you have ever had but it doesn't work out and you are left asking yourself how you could be so stupid. He was married but you refused to let your attraction get in the way of something so trivial.

Sexual tension can be an overwhelming force but it doesn't have to be negative like the above story. Rather, you can harness this tool to create attraction in others as well as understanding your own and avoiding situations that will inevitably cause you pain.

Tension is a good thing!

Please understand that tension doesn't have to be negative, tension is simply the expression of power perceived by the opposite sex as attractive. Here are some more examples of what positive tension can be:

- Beauty
- Intelligence
- Confidence
- Fearlessness
- Kindness

63

- Fitness
- Sexuality
- Creativity

When you excel in one of these categories and you are proud and unapologetic of who you are, this creates tension for the person that may not excel to the same degree in that area. When one finds another that has equal power in different areas and mutual respect for the others qualities you have a level of tension that can lead to a long very exciting relationship.

It is your job to make sure that your power is well expressed, that you are proud of it, and that you don't apologize for it. It is also your job to defend your boundaries, your sense of right and wrong without anger or self-doubt. It is your job to be comfortable in your own skin and radiate the level of confidence great enough to attract someone worthy of you.

So Mike, if I'm strong and confident in my beauty and sexuality, and my guy is stronger in his confidence and fearlessness, then this a good tension? A match made in heaven?!

Hahaha, I am afraid it is more complicated than that. This is because you have to perceive the balance instinctually; you have to get a feel for it. It is also not as cut and dry as a couple of different qualities. Strong healthy sexual tension is as fleeting and confusing as the movement of a school of fish. Fortunately though, you have a brilliant sensor, your brain! All you have to do is teach (unteach??) it what to look for and let it do the work for you. That killer partner is much closer than you think.

Maintaining sexual tension with Power Balance

Every relationship demands balance because without it tension no longer exists and without tension there is boredom. This is ultimately the reason for the failure of most relationships including friendships. When I explain this concept to most people they baulk because they seem to think that tension is a negative quality, but nothing could be further from the truth. The reason we need tension is because we need to grow, we become better people when we are with someone that pushes our worldview or just balances out our poor behavior.

I have an excellent friend of mine in Southern California. He is a very very intelligent guy that looks like a member of the Hells Angels. Jon affectionately calls me a scrawny noodle armed tree-hugger. (In my defense I am 6 foot and 190 pounds) Why are we friends? Because we push each other's boundaries in a way that is respectful and encourages mutual growth. If at one point I have learned all I can from Jon or one of us damages the balance the friendship will end. This is identical to the relationship with the opposite sex and unless it is maintained and nurtured, it will fail.

The Teeter-Totter

Too much positive tension

Imagine you are standing on a teeter-totter with your partner. Now picture yourself taking a large step towards them, if they don't move what will happen? His or her side will head towards the ground, once on the ground your partner might think it is rather boring there and decide to step off. What will happen to you? Well you will go crashing to the ground hard enough to shatter your teeth.

This is what happens when you move aggressively towards or away from your target, you destroy the balance and both of you end up on the ground.

There are tons of ways to maintain and nurture power balance but the truth is that you probably already do most of them with your friends and family. All you need to do is learn to apply them a little bit more towards the opposite sex and realize that the maintenance of balance in a physical relationship is ten times more important than you once thought

66

To understand power balance a little better here is a video on how the attraction is affected when you move forward or back in the balance.

Video: Sexual Tension and Power balance
http://vimeo.com/19971047

Sexual Tension examples

Many men and the typical Pick Up Artist is able to succeed because he creates a negative tension with a woman. He often creates attraction by aggressively making fun of her in a way she cannot easily defend. This ego rape is a negative tension and one that can't be maintained. He will inevitably bore of her and move on to his next target in order to support his sex, new woman habit. Not a positive cycle but it illustrates the negative addictive side of sexual tension.

How about the woman that follows "The rules." She is creating a form of tension as well by forcing the man to wait and pursue. What happens when he finally lands his prey? The sexual tension is often broken and things fade UNLESS in the waiting a new tension was created. Something like mutual respect and enjoyment of the other person but more often than not the only tension was sexual.

How about the really really nice guy? He buys the girl flowers and calls her 4 times a day. There is no tension here and unless she is doing exactly the same thing the relationship will fail due to boredom on her part and the guy will be all butt-hurt because "the nice guy never wins" This is bullshit of course, the proper belief is, "The ass kisser never wins." It is perfectly okay to be a nice

67

guy (girl) as long as you can sense the balance and back off when it is appropriate.

Now the typical girl that falls in love with every guy she meets and is constantly crushed because men are all bastards. She meets a cool guy, resists for a week or two and then finally explodes with passion and screws his brains out. She now completely loses mental control and thinks she is part of the cast of Titanic. She comes on WAY too strong and takes one giant step forward on the teeter-totter and... His side goes crashing to the ground. The balance is crushed and the guy unfairly takes the rap.

These are wonderful examples. This idea of tension is one of the main things that I impress upon my clients. Don't call him. Don't offer to split the meal on the first date. Don't have sex on the first date (or second, or third). Don't ask him out. Why? Because you're offering no tension! Most men will not be intrigued for long by a woman who offers up everything on a silver platter. Remember when I told you earlier about always being so nice? I offered the men in my dating life (and marriage) no tension. Don't you find a guy a lot more interesting if he isn't trying to fulfill your every desire? Challenge is interesting ladies! Don't deny him, or yourself the amazing excitement a little resistance creates.

Maintaining the balance

How many relationships older than 5 years do you know that are still successful? 1 or 2? None? Does this tell you something? It is extremely difficult for a long-term relationship to stay exciting or to maintain balance. I am a skeptic but at the same time I do think the only way to make a run at things is through understanding balance and learning to maintain it.

68

A long time ago something changed when I lost 20 pounds and started to model in LA. My girlfriend and best friend of two years suddenly didn't want to touch me. She complained that my shoulder was too boney to sleep on. She tried to get me to eat junk food and would buy my favorite beer and drink it in front of me. Not long after, she cheated on me and we separated.

What happened? The balance was shaken, I lost weight, and she felt insecure about this and the possible beautiful women I would meet. The relationship was sabotaged by her and permanently ruined.

If the concepts of sexual tension and power balance are not stamped to your brain, go back and read this chapter again! Draw a little teeter-totter and imagine what will happen if you say, "I love you" before he is ready to take that step. If it is not obvious what will happen when:

- You come on too strong
- You call him at 3 am (or every day)
- You cook him dinner without him reciprocating
- You sleep with him even though he says he is not interested in anything else
- You never push him, challenge him or set boundaries

Don't get it, read this chapter again!

Ladies, take note of what Mike just told you...he basically just handed you wisdom wrapped in a 24k gold box with a diamond bow, in other words a pretty spectacular gift! Don't initiate or take the lead. Let the guy do it. Don't call or text him unless he's called or texted you first. He hasn't contacted you in 4 days? You automatically jump to, "What if something's happened to him? What if he's too busy to call? Wouldn't it be nice if I just sent a text to let him know I'm thinking about him?" Stop it!

Cut the crap and wake up! Ladies! He doesn't want to talk to you! If he did he would've called, texted, or sent a homing pigeon with a message strapped to its foot. He'll call you when he wants to talk to you. Men are not women. In the beginning of a relationship they have no need to chat with us everyday for no reason. **Most importantly, they need some space to realize that they miss us.** There will be no tension if you're always up under him, saying hi, cooking him dinner, giving up the goodies (sex). He will have all the power and no sexual tension, which means he won't find you as attractive or mysterious. You will come off as needy. And who wants that?

Do you see the line above in bold? This was a gift from Kim, and it's beautiful in it's truth and simplicity

"Most importantly, they need some space to realize that they miss us."

Could you do this for us men??? Please? Please, please please!?? I really really enjoy being attracted to you, and when you are impatient, I lose my attraction, just give me that little bit of time to miss you. It would make a world of difference for **us** and I am not exaggerating.

Conditions necessary for strong sexual tension:
•

• Independent strength – you are strong and you do not need the other's strength to survive.

- • Intelligence – equal and balanced, both of you look up to the other.
- • Opinionated – Lovers don't need to have the same worldview; in fact to push your partner to a new understanding of the world is a beautiful gift.
- • Demanding of respect – Without this, no love can maintain. You must be willing to lose what you love in order to protect who you are.
- • Continuous desire for growth – This must be present and equal in both partners, you don't need to be moving in the same direction but you must be moving at the same speed.
- • Equal physical/sexual attraction – If you can look at your lover and say, "My god... is that who I am going to make love to tonight?" Wow, is there any greater positive sexual tension than this?
- • Intellectual connection – Intelligence is not enough, you must love and enjoy the beautiful pattern of thought the other person weaves, knitting yourself into their being.
- • Fun, Humor and delight – Without laughter and joy, what relationship can be whole?
- • Communication – This is the glue that binds your resonance, without it your pattern will unravel and the connection will be lost. It is a skill and one you have to constantly maintain.

Sexual tension is about balance, a delightful crackling of power and respect. Finding this positive tension starts with you, for what positive relationship can be fostered if negative is in your resonance.

Below is possibly one of the best stories I have ever written, about how relationships bind together. I hope you take the time to read it. - Mike

Needle in a haystack – finding the perfect man
By Mike Masters

Seriously? You want to marry her?

I got into horrible trouble after a conversation, with my sister's psycho ex-boyfriend. "Dude, stop. I know you are in love with my sister, but seriously? Come on buddy. There are two types of girls in the world: the ones that you marry and the ones that you sleep with. Honestly, which one do you think my sister is??" As you can imagine I got in a whole lot of trouble for this one.

My friend Jen is really frustrated, she is caught between two guys. One is the Sportsfish and the other is the Keeper. I didn't know this terminology until Jen explained it too me, "It is from the comedian Steve Harvey, who wrote the book, Act Like a Lady, Think Like a Man. "Hmmm..." I said, "That sounds a lot like my theory of the Nester and the Breeder." I haven't read his book but the analogy is excellent so I am going to steal it to explain something I seriously doubt Steve does.

There are two states that nearly all of the people we are attracted to fall under. The Sportsfish and the Keeper. The Sportfish is the exciting and unobtainable guy/girl, they are incredibly fun and slightly out of our reach. The Keeper represents safety and security, and are too easily reached, and eventually become boring.

Simple? Really...? Lets add a few layers of complexity.

1.   Everyone, including you, has the capacity to be a Sportsfish or a Keeper
2.   The others perception of you pushes you to either state
3.   We often try to force the Sportsfish into the role of the Keeper (chill out Captain Ahab)
4.   After being burned by the Sportfish many of us flee to the Keeper (then we cheat on them)
5.   There are apparent conflicting demands of human nature, we want the Sportsfish that is a Keeper

This is one of the things that makes it so frustrating to be human. We live fricken forever, we need to be paired to raise our young, and we have a ridiculously over developed mind that revels in throwing monkey wrenches into the cogs of its evolutionary programming. We are probably

72

the only animal that enters the world so bloody confused over the opposite sex.

The failure pattern

I am no exception and I did what most people do. I attempted to land the Sportsfish for most of my life. I lived for the danger and the excitement, I LOVED the chase and the attempts at taming this feral beast but I got cut, slashed, hurt. I bled with tears and frustration over the need for security and mental health, I screamed on the inside for something simple, normal and tame. What did I do? Exactly what you did or are going to do soon. I found "the Keeper" and? I got so bloody bored that I vomited peace and calm all over the shoes of my security.

There are a few phases of maturity that people go through with relationships. Maybe they start from the direction of security or the exciting side of danger. Whichever side they start from they will oscillate from one to the other. They will use one failure to prove to themselves that the opposite must be the solution, which of course in its failure will point back to the next extreme.

The understanding of this dichotomy is the second stage of relationship maturity. It is when one realizes that they need both the Sportsfish and the Keeper to be happy.

Life and the perfect wave

There is a secret to life that parallels all relationships: life is not static nor should it be. There is no destination, everything in life is a vision that we put into motion, flowing over the completion of that vision with the next. With life, the secret to incredible passion and Joy is riding the cusp of one's comfort zone, riding it as a surfer would a wave. This comfort zone will ebb, flow and oscillate and you must be willing to limberly dance on its edge.

Attempting to land the Sportsfish is the same as the surfer dropping into a wave much too big for him or her. It will tumble them every time. The Keeper wave is equally as disappointing and can't challenge the surfer's abilities or help them grow. The perfect wave is the one that rides the cusp of your abilities. It is that perfect combination of safety and danger. This is what is sexy, this is what makes life worth living!

However, there is a complication, you are both on a wave, you are both surfing the other, and are both dynamic in your enjoyment. You are the generator of your partner's wave, and are the one that keeps the challenge and safety in balance. When relationships crumble it is most inevitably because the balance of each other's wave was never correct OR that balance was compromised during your time together. The wave you create for your partner is your responsibility, and the one they create for you, must be demanded.

It is this magical balance that you are seeking and it is a magical balance that you bring to the table for them. This is a tightrope of qualities and challenges constantly shifting in all parties. It is an organic thing that can only be harnessed by its organic equal.

Finding the perfect wave

We all have the intrinsic need to ride the perfect wave and we must ride many waves to know who or what that person is. We will also be ridden, leaving people lacking or tumbling into the foam. This is the natural progression, and it is incredibly elusive, it is the bull's eye on the back of a wild horse. Yes, it is challenging, yes it is scary, but can you honestly tell yourself that you would have it any other way? Could that partnership ever be so wonderfully beautiful if it didn't take all your skill to master it? No, you must be responsible for finding the sweet spot in that relationship wave. You must never give up or settle for someone too strong or too weak. The perfect wave is out there, and as you drop in they will do the same, creating an ecstasy in union as you ride the cusp of each other's delicious slopes.

VII. Setting your intention - Know what you want

"How can anyone hit a target they cannot see?" – Zig Zigglar

Clearly defining what you do and don't want

I used to race bicycles in Japan, this meant that I was on busy surface streets with thousands of cars. Everyday I would saddle up on a pinprick of a seat in padded tight cycling gear. The second I pulled off my street my attitude would change radically; traffic was the enemy, drivers and taxis out to get me. I would ride the 25 miles to work 4-5 days a week as the crazed gaijin, weaving in and out of a sea of Toyotas. People would pull out in front of me, try to beat me to a signal or just turn into me. For years I would rage at them, swearing in English and later Japanese.

After two years of this battle a disturbing revelation came to me. It happened when a taxi pulled in front of me and I bellowed at him. Then I saw the driver's face, it was shocked and shaken, he was honestly scared. With wet fingers the candle of my anger went out and it hit me... I realized in profound sadness, I was responsible.

When I replayed the movie in my mind, I realized I had seen the taxi about to pull out and I purposely got in his way so I could yell at him. I hadn't realized that I did this until I saw the pain on his face. I caused this, I created this controversy, I was the one that wanted to shake my self-righteous fist at the heathen driver.

From that point on I took a completely different view towards the drivers in Japan and shockingly in the next 2 years of cycling. I never had one accident or skirmish. I had no idea how responsible I was for the world around me.

Guiding your intention

I do not believe in a literal "Secret" like manifestation of thoughts into reality. Why? Simply because I spent years trying to implement the "law of attraction" but found it would only work 50% of the time. In retrospect this was a very good thing or I would have years ago been a very unhappy but wealthy man with no idea that his passion is writing. Therefore, if I believe the law of attraction is not a LAW in the slightest, and that getting everything you want is a short cut to misery, why write this chapter?

Setting your intention is very different than the law of attraction. Imagine you plan a trip, you plan every last detail, and everything works flawlessly. Was this a good trip? Were there any unknowns? Is this a good thing? Is it even possible? Now imagine a trip with no destination, you just walk into an airport, throw your money down and see what happens. While this might be incredibly exciting, what if you landed in Bosnia? Or the Artic? Would you be prepared for this? Would it be in line with what you wanted? Probably not.

This is why we are going to plan our trip, throw down some details, make some requests and then divorce ourselves from the results. We surrender to the adventure; we allow life to return the results that we truly want. What? What we truly want? Yup, I would argue that you don't really know what you truly want and by letting go of the wheel of control we can allow life to guide us in the direction that is more appropriate. So... I want you to define the target, I want you to look for it but I also want you to relinquish control and be willing to flow with what life is going to throw at you. If your results are not what you wanted, take what you have learned and draw a new target, and surrender again. Repeat, life long.

How critical this is in relationships

The world you manifest is a reflection of what is inside of you. If you are foul inside, you will attract all that is foul. If you hate men and think they are scum, you will draw them like cockroaches so you can have the pleasure of squashing them. You will bring into your life any and all, that support your mental composite of the world.

To prove this to yourself all one has to do is take a look at your drama queen friends to see how this works. Is it not remarkable how they seem to draw nightmares? Is this because they are cursed or because they actually are valuing and protecting this aspect of their life? Without these experiences they would be forced to become a different person, which of course they have no desire to become. So in other words, they are requesting the trip to Bosnia, just so they can bitch and moan about how awful it was.

Do I have to gut you and your thinking to create change? Almost, hahaha but hopefully not, all we need do is take baby steps in the direction we want and constantly reinforce and redefine, but this will never happen until we first know what we want.

Get clear and avoid what you don't want

On my bicycle I knew that I hated rude selfish drivers but instead of being repelled by them I was drawn into their dance and we would tango in anger. Later, I focused on wanting a great workout and a fun ride to work. The rude drivers were still very much there but I would not dance; it was shocking how effortless it was to go around the person ready to cut me off, or smile at the taxi trying to beat me to the turn. I was finally clear about what I wanted and what I didn't want, I avoided the negative easily without a second thought.

Do you get how powerful this is? The principle that feelings and thoughts can attract things into your life is amazing. In relationships if you feel men are only out for one thing and manipulative scum that is what you will get in your life. If you have the positive thought and more importantly start to feel that men are wonderful, respectful, and treat you with love and kindness *that* is what you'll get in your life!

Let me give you a weird example of how this happened in my life. When I started dating, I would always date outside of my race. Plenty of white, Indian, Latino, and Asian men would ask me out but no black men. I wasn't upset about this (my sister calls me the United Nations of dating!) but thought this was a bit strange since I love black men and wanted a little chocolate in my life too!

I started examining what was going on in my thoughts to omit an entire race of men from my dating experience. I realized that I was focused on a particular statistic that stated that the

78

black population in my city was less than 7% and diminishing. Take into consideration that the number gets smaller once you account for women, children, married black men, gay black men, and older than I want to date black men-I started thinking I was never going to find any black men to date! I internalized this and took on the thought and feeling that there weren't any black men in my city! So what happened? I didn't date black men because I told myself they weren't there!

Once I figured out what my thoughts were attracting (or not attracting) into my life I started changing my feelings. I told myself there were plenty of handsome, smart, eligible black men in my city. Guess what happened? You got it; these awesome men started popping into my life: I'd see a gorgeous black man at a fundraiser; would meet a black Harvard grad at dinner with friends; would chat with an unmarried black guy at the Laundromat.

My point is what you think about, you bring about. My next mission is to bring a tall cute Frenchmen who cooks for me!

What Do you Want? What Don't you Want?

Want to access that big brain of yours? Hands down the best way is the exercise of listing. If you seriously want to move on and have a better life and a better partner it is crucial for you to figure out exactly what you do and don't want. Why is this so important? Because... **often we are very vague about what we do and don't want which leads us into the same traps over and over again.**

If you want to reorganize a room, the proper way to do it is to first get everything the hell out of that room, and I mean EVERYTHING. Once it is all out we can figure out what is junk that we need to trash and what we

79

need to keep. That is what listing does, it pulls all the thoughts out of your head and puts them on the table for you to organize and focus on.

Trust me on this one, the typical, "Yeah... I know what I want" is complete manure. Once you list things out you will see that there is a lot more trapped in your head.

To really change for the better you must learn to clearly define what you do and do not want. Imagine Santa Clause, God, or some matchmaker with a 100% success rate has told you to list 10 things you want in a man. Anything from: I want a man who's a great kisser, to I want a man who owns his own business. I guarantee once you get in the flow, listing 20, 50 or 100 things you want in a man will be easy. So do it. No one has to see the list but you.

The second advantage to listing is that it makes your brain face/accept issues that it might be avoiding. It makes the problem/solution more concrete and thus allows you to act on it. Don't pass this exercise up!

Grab a piece of paper, or open up Microsoft Word and start listing! I would like you to hit a minimum of 20, there are no wrong answers, set a time limit of 10 minutes and just let loose.

What I do NOT want in my next relationship?

1. A man not willing to listen to me (doesn't contact me regularly... every day/every other day)
2. Abuse of any kind (physical, emotional, verbal, sexual)
3. A partner not generous in bed (selfish lover)
4. Racist or sexist
5. A weak willed guy that lets me walk on him
6. Too short (shorter than me)

7. A man with lots of female "friends"
8. Dishonesty, even the slightest
9. Smoker
10. Abuses alcohol or drugs
11. Doesn't respect my spirituality
12. Doesn't like to try new things
13. Man who doesn't enjoy socializing
14. Man who doesn't value family and friends
15. Man who cheats on me
16. Doesn't appreciate me
17. Sarcastic to the point of being hurtful
18. Bad with finances
19. A man who doesn't like dogs
20. A man who is arrogant

Done? Did you make it to 20? If not please complete this; the last 5 are the ones that have a tendency to glimpse into your soul.

Santa Cares, Really!

So that list is done. Santa, God, or the 100% Success Matchmaker needs to know what you DON'T want! Santa may say "I've got this great guy I would love to give you for Christmas, but he's mean to the waitresses...is that okay?" God taps you on the shoulder and says "I'm thinking of setting you up with this handsome MBA from Harvard who loves children and kittens but I didn't know if his smoking cigarettes only when he drinks is a deal breaker or not for you. Should I hook it up? 100% Matchmaker calls you one day and says, "The 6'2" billionaire who cares for his ailing grandmother, is all set to commit and marry you but he cheated on his ex-wife...numerous times. I didn't think this would matter, but wanted to check with you first. You good with that?"

The point of your Divorce Guru's above fantasy is that it's important to know what you do want, and equally, if not MORE importantly, to know what you don't want. I don't want someone who can't love my boys, support my spirituality or has dirt under his nails at dinner. We cannot stress enough how important it is for you to know what you don't want.

What DO you want in your next relationship?

So let's flip-flop it! This is a lot easier to do now that we have the negative list to work off of. Initially, I would like you to not use any of your negative list to create your positive one. When you start slowing down, then look at the negative and flip it into something positive.

Example: A man not willing to listen => I am with a guy that listens with compassion and understanding.

Okay let's make the second list

Who and what do I want in my next relationship?

1. Shows his love with tokens and gifts (flowers, cards, jewelry, hand written notes, text to let me know he's thinking of me)
2. He is comfortable and gets along well with my family, friends and co-workers
3. He is wonderful in bed and satisfies my sexual needs
4. He knows I'm a catch and is proud to have me on his arm
5. He is the perfect height and dresses perfectly for my tastes
6. I trust him completely/He is faithful
7. He is athletic and healthy
8. We share similar religious beliefs
9. Is involved in his community (volunteer work, boards, tutoring etc.)
10. He is well read

11. Enjoys culture (museums, art galleries, ballet etc.)
12. Treats people with respect
13. Ambitious /Hard working
14. Strong and confident
15. Visionary
16. Charismatic and friendly
17. Open minded
18. Enjoys world travel
19. Enjoys a variety of food
20. Has a wonderful family that totally accepts me

I assume you finished and got to #20 just like the negative list. This is your map to the destination you desire. This is the ticket you are buying, it may not be all you desire but if not, we can make a new list and a new destination.

Obviously, we are going to ignore the negative since we don't want to get that but we still want to be aware of it. The positive list is what we want to really put our focus on, since this is our target. This list needs to be posted somewhere you can see so you can fire at it daily. You must burn this list into your head and start giving guidance to what you want in a relationship.

Please remember this is not magic, it is simply a changing and sharpening of your focus.

More resources on attraction/intention:
What The Bleep Do We Know
http://www.whatthebleep.com/
Abraham-Hicks
http://www.abraham-hicks.com/lawofattractionsource/index.php
Seen all of the above and want a really mind blowing book?
Busting loose from the money game –

http://www.amazon.com/Busting-Loose-Money-Game-Mind-Blowing/dp/0470047496 (It really isn't about money)

VIII. Getting your game on – Confidence is key

Let's assume that you get the above chapters, that you feel ready to find the right guy. However, there is one thing missing, Action! Now it is time to put the pedal to the pavement but first we need to start the car! To do so we need to have faith we need to trust we need to believe that we know what we are doing. To do this takes a leap of faith and that faith is rooted in confidence. It's okay if you don't feel it now but you will, later you wont have any doubts that you are on the right path.

Now that you have determined that you are ready to date after your heart has been ground into the dirt, let me talk to you about the most important word you will need to know before going out into the jungle of the dating world armed with intention. First you need... Confidence.

Confidence

You may be saying, yeah Kim, I've got confidence. What I need is a new wardrobe, some sexy shoes, an expensive haircut, liposuction, collagen injections, a gym membership, and a 6 month membership to J-Date. I say no you don't because you could have all of these things, plus the body of a Victoria Secret model but without confidence, you ain't goin' very far.

Don't underestimate what a strong level of confidence will do for you. Confidence will remind you that you've got it going on even if you don't always feel like you do. Confidence will attract

85

the man that you want, versus the men that you don't want. Confidence will have you believe that there ain't no mountain high enough…ain't no river wide enough…ain't no valley low enough to keep me from getting…wait, I'm singing a Diana Ross song. To sum it up, without confidence you will not believe in yourself. You will not love yourself. And if you don't love you, who will?

A little Confidence test

You say you have confidence already? Okay, let's put your money where your mouth is.

- You get a free ticket to a posh fundraiser where there will be great food, great wine, and lots of successful and eligible bachelors. You have no one to accompany you. Do you go get dressed up, slip on some stilettos and go solo?

OR

- Stay home and spend a fattening evening with two guys named Ben and Jerry?

You are perusing your online dating profile and notice that a very cute guy has checked out your profile but has not written. Do you:

- Write him a quick witty note letting him know that you think his love of stadium mustard and eggplant is endearing and not to be shy about writing you next time he checks out your profile?

OR

- Do you: assume that he must not have written you for a reason. Maybe he doesn't want to date you because you're divorced, have kids, and likes long walks on the beach?

You just woke up and are headed out to get a bagel. You haven't showered and you're wearing ugg boots because they are comfortable. While waiting for the light to turn green, you realize that the man in the dapper suit standing in front of you is the handsome guy named Greg you met at the Laundromat 3 weeks earlier who uses the expensive organic laundry detergent. Do you:

• Put your head down and hope he doesn't notice you because instead of sexy attire and lipstick you're wearing ugly lime green boots and a sweatshirt?

OR

• Do you playfully say, "My, don't we look handsome today Greg? Didn't realize you cleaned up so well!

This, my fellow separated comrade, is a test of your self-confidence. I don't think I need to tell you (you are a smart woman after all!) that if you answered yes to the first choices, you are a confident woman that no divorce or any other hardship could ever diminish. Rock on girlfriend! If you answered yes to one or more of the second choices...well, stick with me and you will learn how to be so confident in who you are that not even a pair of lime green UGG boots can stop you from a little sidewalk flirting!

Let me say this: confidence isn't just for hooking a man. It's needed to deal with your new life. If your man cheated on you, you need confidence to know that it wasn't because you were fatter, older, or not as attractive as that hussy he's with now. Well it might be because of these reasons. But with confidence you will realize that even the most beautiful and thin women get cheated on. Hello paging Jennifer Anniston! Repeat after me...Halle Berry. Pamela Anderson. Kim Hess (uh, that's me).

These 3 women have their cheating exes in common with me, but more importantly they also have confidence in common.

Confidence to move on from their married lives, and on to live better lives. The confidence to have their sniveling, cheating husbands look at them in amazement and regret the day they ever said less than kind words to you. Knowing that you are surviving-no, THRIVING-without them. It happens…just read the tabloids and my blog! My ex is like "WTF, she's happier and more confident without me!" Boo-yah.

It happened to me too

Note: all three of these scenarios happened to Kim Hess your Divorce Guru…(and yes, I do own a pair of lime green UGG boots. They're comfortable and they were on sale!) I'm sure I don't have to tell you (once again, you're a smart gal!) that I chose all three of the "confident" choices. I ended up getting drunk at the fundraiser and meeting awesome new friends, got 6 months of great sex out of the second scenario, and really did tell Greg the laundry guy that he looked great in a suit. Now every time he sees me he gives me a big goofy grin. But ladies, I have not always chosen the confident choices. I was not always the confident divorce diva you have in front of you today. My lack of confidence was attracting to me exactly what I thought I was worth: crap.

Shockingly, confidence can and will trump raw sex appeal every time. The super sexy girl without confidence might get sex but she will never get a relationship. The average, uber confident girl however… totally different story. This is the kind of girl a man can take seriously. This kind of girl is the one that takes all the quality guys off the market. Confidence is built by being willing to make mistakes, willing to be put through the mill and still bounce back.

Confidence is an unshakable belief in one's self that is so great, no man can dent it. Confidence is true beauty.

Amen Mike!

Applying confidence to your intention

You want that amazing sexy, smart, powerful man? Ladies, like attracts like! You believe you are sexy, smart, and a great catch, then you will attract a man who is sexy, smart, and a great catch. If you believe that you're dumpy, unattractive, dull, and that no one good will want you, who do you think will be attracted to you? Yep, you got it…those men who sit in front of the TV or computer screen twelve hours a day in their mom's basement, scratching their belly and substituting Twinkies for their daily recommended allowance of fruit and vegetables. Get my drift?

Having confidence gets you what you want. Having confidence shows you what you deserve…and you always deserve the best. Set your intention to be the best, which will attract to you the best. If you focus on being who you want to be, then you will attract the best men, the dates, the best sex and the best relationships that are out there, but first you must set your intention on what you want to attract.

When I got clear on the type of woman I wanted to be (in case you're wondering, a prosperous, sexy, confident, playful, spiritually, mentally, and physically healthy woman) it forced me to get clear on the type of man I wanted to date and be in my life: a prosperous, sexy, confident, playful, spiritually, mentally, and physically healthy man. Before I set my intention on who I wanted to spend my precious time and energy on I was getting all kinds of crappy men and didn't know why. Those who had low self-esteem, no goals or directions, spiritually corrupt, lacked confidence in their abilities, and who chose to live a lifestyle of lack and poverty.

89

XI. Sure I am confident, but I don't feel sexy

Now that we know what we want, becoming the woman you want to be to attract a high quality guy is the next step, so let's move on to sexy time! " But wait," oh wise Divorce Guru and magnificent Master Dater, you're shouting, "My body looks waaayyy different than it did 10 years ago."

This is something very personal for almost every person going through divorce or a bad break up has to face. You've been with the same guy for Lord knows how long. He's seen you gain weight, he's seen you in your granny period panties, and he's seen you naked. Admit it, you've let yourself go. Relationships will do that. We eat a lot, we gain weight, we get lazy and stop working out. Now it's time to get that healthy sexy bod back.

Single people have a lot of incentive to be sexy and stay that way. Getting back out in the single crowd feeling confident can be a little intimidating, especially if the last time you were out there you were 30 pounds lighter and had no stretch marks.

Mike how did ya know?! When I left the dating game I was 22. Yep, 22 with a flat tummy, tight butt, no jiggle to my wiggle, no stretch marks and thong panties. Well, at 35, I gotta be honest, the only thing left to Kim at 22 are the thongs.

I've had two kids. With childbirth came stretch marks and an ability to pack on 5 lbs just smelling a bacon cheeseburger. And what do I say to this? Don't let it be an excuse. Sexy comes in all shapes and sizes. Some men like their woman tight and firm.

Some men like their women with a little something extra to hold on to. But who cares what some men like? I'm here to let you know what YOU like is the most important thing. Here we go with the confidence again.

Ever see a...um..."heavier" woman with a tight dress on, rolls spilling out all over? Of course you have, we all have unfortunately! But let's learn a lesson from this woman. She likes her body. She likes her body so much that she wants to show it to the world. Should she show it to the world? That's another book! But she loves her body, no matter what flaws she is supposed to be ashamed of. I'm not telling you to wear ill-fitting clothes that don't flatter you. What I am telling you is that your body has a right not to look like it did 10 years ago. Even supermodels, weight conscious actresses, and female athletes don't have the same bodies they had 10 years ago. Go with it. Enjoy your body as is. If you love it, or at least can find the sexy and good parts of your body, I can 100% guarantee you that a great majority of the men you date will find the parts you find good or decent positively sexy and irresistible! But, I guarantee that you will find your body that much better and appealing if you work at keeping it in tip top condition.

Now let's get the opinion of a man. Oh, Miiikkkeee....

Being sexy is relative

This is a tough one! And one I am very biased about. I am a nutritionist and worked for years as a personal trainer and one truth I have learned over the years is that people are a lot happier being in better shape. Which of course is also very relative, so what I mean is, in shape for YOU.

People that eat well and exercise:

- They feel more confident in all areas of life.
- They suffer less depression
- They get sick less often
- They have a better sex life
- They encourage their children to do the same
- Blah
- blah
- blah

You're probably saying "I've heard this a million times over and over...who fricken' cares?! Except for one simple fact:

"Guys are simple creatures that are initially more attracted to the physical than the mental"

Let me translate this into woman talk: Your potential dating pool of guys absolutely cares!

Sure, there are many exceptions to this rule but don't you want to give yourself the best chance possible to meet a great guy?

I myself think there are NO exceptions to this rule (with a normal man with no self esteem issues!) Take a genius, charming, kind woman who is overweight, frumpy and wears sweats every day, and an equally genius, charming, kind woman who exercises and takes pride in her appearance and you tell me who the guy is going to pick?

So suck it up and use your need to meet a sexy guy fuel you to do something you should be doing anyway. After you find and commit to the perfect guy, you have my permission to get fat.

Ladies, let me jump in here and say IF you commit to the perfect guy (you might be perfectly happy never committing and never having to pick up dirty underwear off the floor !)

Get in shape again, do it now. Call your fit girlfriend and ask her to take you to the gym tomorrow. (You know, the one you secretly hate who wears a size 4, eats brown rice and complains about her fat thighs and how she needs to add an extra 3 miles on the 6 miles she runs every day? Yeah, call her.) **Don't wait to do this, stop and do it now!!!**

I am a nutritionist and I am convinced that many different approaches work for weight loss and health.

More of a carnivore? The book Protein Power is excellent
http://www.amazon.com/Protein-Power-High-Protein-Carbohydrate-Health/dp/0553574752
Want a more tree huggy approach? Diet for a New America is perfect
http://www.amazon.com/Diet-New-America-John-Robbins/dp/0915811812/ref=sr_1_1?ie=UTF8&s=books&qid=1275409920&sr=1-1
I am also very impressed with Tim Ferris' newest book Four hour body he has done is homework and I can't poke holes in his argument.
http://www.amazon.com/4-Hour-Body-Incredible-Superhuman-ebook/dp/B003EI2EH2
(These are not affiliate links)

X. Getting good at the game - How to kill the competition

I could write 10 e-books on the art of the game but since we don't really have time for this I will do my best to hit a couple of problem areas. I would ask you to trust me here. I know a few of you will have resistance to the concept of "the game" so if need be change the word "game" in your mind to "compatibility testing" (but since that sounds kinda lame I won't use it).

The game is not played so that you can win; it is played for fun, to build attraction, and to test compatibility. We have no desire to crush our opponent but we need to understand a little strategy so that we can actually return a serve and have a good volley.

Fortunately, you already understand sexual tension and power balance (right??). These are more important than any of the ideas below, why? Because all of my little tips and tricks are stemmed from sexual tension and power balance. If you understand these earlier concepts, you will see how insignificant "rules" are. However, before you run you must walk, so for the time being don't violate anything below!

In this chapter we will jump around a few areas of the "game" and expand on things that are more important for people recovering from a breakup. The purpose of this chapter is to make you immediately aware of some of the more important parts of the relationship game, without getting overly detailed. We had fun writing it hope you enjoy reading it.

The Game - Tips to ensure your success

Never be needy

The number one turn off for everyone is a needy partner. This lack of strength works to repel men as effectively as a vegetarian pizza served with non-alcoholic beer. (What? guys don't like veggie pizza and beer that won't get you buzzed?) Needy behavior is: jealousy, nosiness, needing to control, emotional freak-outs, stupid questions (Where is this relationship going?) dishonesty, did I mention jealousy??? Don't do this under pain of getting: Used, ignored, cheated on, left and other generally bad things.

We've all had that girlfriend that complains to us about her man. She whines, she cries, she goes on and on about the fight that she started last night. She gets mad if he goes out with friends, she breaks into his email, and she needs him to be by her side 24 hours a day. You see in her the jealousy, the nosiness, the need to control her man-and it's disgusting. Not a good look huh? You want to tell her to get a life and stop needing to be in his life so damn much!

If it doesn't look good on her, it's not going to look good on you. Get a life outside of the man you're dating so you won't be needy towards him. Neediness is so uncool.

Step up and be a man!

But I am a woman??? I hope so... but that is not really what I mean. What I mean is taking on the male roll. Do

95

you remember Samantha from Sex in the City? She was a great example of this, she was a man-eater and they loved her for it. This may not be your bag but if it sings to you, it might be wonderful for your confidence to get out there and flex your kegel muscles again.

Crappy Communication kills

You ladies are so much better at communication than most men but when it comes to that guy you like, the pleaser or the evil bitch comes out. Funny how when we actually care about someone we lose all ability to communicate rationally, either we are busy trying destroy the relationship out of a deep-seated self loathing OR we are destroying their respect for us by trying to please them. The key problem here is that emotions are sabotaging our ability to say and do the right thing but at least awareness is the first step.

Vulnerability is courageous

You are a confident rock! An island of power!! No man can ever hurt you again!!! This is not at all where I want you to end up, these are walls and as walls they keep people out. If you really want to be powerful you must lay yourself open to attack, you must trust. Showing your vulnerability is like opening your home to a stranger. Sure, once in a while someone might steal a cd or a beer out of the fridge but most will respect what you have done. Being vulnerable is about tearing down those walls and facing your fears, it is about communication and honesty. I know it is counterintuitive but true strength starts here.

Don't play at being a hard ass all the time. What, are you in prison? Men truly like softness and needing to be needed by

96

you. It truly is okay to open up and let your man know you aren't made of concrete. Even the strongest woman needs a shoulder to lean on. Let a man know he is a man by being vulnerable at times and leaning on him. He'll be happy and you'll be happy!

Playful, funny bratty

After such heavy topics this one has a bit more levity! This is a key to catching and keeping his interest. Being playful, funny, bratty is your fencing sword, it is the weapon you will use to challenge him, to make him step up and take notice of you. Being playful and funny can rarely be criticized and screams intelligence if you are talented at it.

The happy bitch

My friend Tamara gets away with MURDER, she can slap guys in the face and give them hell. To most people's shock the guys follow her around like puppies. Personally, I never let her behave this way around me but I still enjoy what is looming under the surface. Tamara is a happy bitch, not an angry one! This kind of behavior may make you uncomfortable at first but it is shocking how effective it can be to get and keep a guys attention.

Busy as a BEEE

"Hey what are you doing tonight?" he asked. "I am free, what are you thinking about doing?" she incorrectly answered. NO NO NO!! What, are you a convenience to him? Does he not have to show you the same respect he would another love interest? Part of the reason he shows respect to the new love interest is

97

because she is an unknown. Why not maintain that type of feeling with him? Why not remain that unknown? The hunter likes to hunt because the deer is elusive and challenging! Don't throw yourself on his gun.

Yeah girl, don't throw yourself on his gun! That says it all! Ladies, here is another way to explain this. Which is more valuable? Running in to a 7-11 convenience store, grabbing one of those hot dogs that's been sitting under the heat lamp for God knows how long or eating a three course dinner at the restaurant you had to make reservations for and wait a week to enjoy. My fellow divas don't be that shriveled up hot dog! I've been the shriveled up hot dog, and let me tell ya...your guy will be hungry later because you're just a snack. I'm with Mike, make that dude make reservations!

When you date reciprocate

It really really bugs me when a girl keeps a tight fist on her finances and expects me to pay for everything. This communicates clearly to me that she doesn't have respect for me, that she is selfish, and horribly old school. Not okay, if he buys dinner one night, you buy it the next. (But he really should pay for the first date UNLESS you are the one to ask him out)

I agree with Mike. I love when a guy pays on the first date but after that share the love! Know what else you can do? Pay for the tip. Buy a round of drinks. Treat him to dessert after dinner. Paying is empowering!

Let's talk about sex? Let's not...

A good friend of mine keeps sending guys running because she brings up sex WAY to early in the conversation. She does so because she really likes sex

98

and she wants to make sure he doesn't have a small penis. (Seriously) This almost always backfires on her because it changes the guy's perception of the situation. Before she was a relationship candidate but after the sex talk she moves into sexual conquest category and an easy one at that. Don't talk about sex, it is just safer that way.

The friend he's talking about (crying, sniffling, wipes a tear from eye)...is me. Okay, it's not. But there are those of us who bring up sex too early. I've learned my lesson(s)! Though it's 2010 there is still a double standard about this. Is it fair? No. Should you take our advice and not bring up sex early so you won't be considered a ho-bag? Yes. Trust me...my own sister called me a hoochie and she is completely correct, but that doesn't mean I want the whole world to know it!

This ain't gonna get you a good man. It will get you a man who will just call you for the "goodies" but he won't be visiting your grandma with you or going on long **Sunday drives. Trust us: zip the lips when it comes to sexy talk too soon.**

The power of NO Expectations

When I was in high school I wanted one thing, I wanted sex! However I learned a very valuable lesson very quickly; if I had the expectation I would very rarely get what I wanted. I changed my self-talk and was able to remove any and all sexual expectations. What happened? Well I got a whole lot more of what I wanted because I was not pushy in the slightest. You might be wondering what a horny high school boy and you have in common, but age/desire does not matter here. If you have a relationship expectation, you expect him to call, you expect him to care, he inevitably will sense your expectation and go the other direction.

This is called the "Wanting It Tax". This means that the more you want it, the higher the price goes! This is simple economics; if the supply is high the demand goes down. If it is a law for billion dollar world markets, don't you think you supplying too much ass might just equate to him not desiring the surplus you are pushing on him?

It's not "playing hard to get", it's more like "being hard to get!" Think of yourself like a beautiful, rare diamond. Hard to get because it may be one of a kind, you are one of a kind. This makes you and the diamond very valuable causing people to want you and work hard to have you. Angelina Jolie, Marilyn Monroe, Naomi Campbell...they are hard to get and worth the "Wanting It Tax." I say you are too!

Have fun! and be ready to say, NEXT!!!

This process does not have to be a scary journey into the depths of dating hell. It can be really fun and extremely funny, heck I have made dating my career. =) Meeting people and having a good time is a blast but if it's not I move on immediately. Should you actively look for the one?? Only if you really want to, at first I think it is more important to just get back into the mix and see what happens. Maybe life will tell you it is time to focus on yourself and not a man, or maybe all you need is a little companionship?

Remember when you were a teenager or in your early twenties? You weren't concerned with finding "the one", or wondering about commitment. You were free and open to what the dating world had to offer! You went out with a boy to have fun, enjoy some good pizza, and laugh! Resurrect that joyous person you were before the divorce, before the break-up, before dating became so serious. Have some good times, woman, you know you deserve it.

Becoming what you wish to attract

We have talked about this before but it really is worth repeating. It took me a long time to realize that the world was my mirror. Everything that I had inside of my head was being projected out into the real world. My anger, frustration and insecurities were bounced back at me on a regular basis. When I started to work on myself and change the bitterness of my soul, I was amazed at the quality of people who suddenly graced my life. It really is that simple, you want someone wonderful? You better be something wonderful! Time to get your ducks in a row ladies, you attract what you are, NO EXCEPTIONS.

When I was a pathetic mess after my divorce, guess who I attracted? You got it, men who were pathetic messes! The more I valued and loved myself, the better caliber men I attracted. I went from a guy who slept on a mattress on the floor with three roommates to attracting a man who owned his own home, plus two apartment buildings in a two states. Yeah, it really does work!

Necessary Boundaries

Boundaries are not only necessary but they are sexy because it shows your strength. Imagine a guy enters your clean home with muddy boots on. Do you let him walk around on your white carpet, or do you say, "Hey! Brainless wonder!! Take your damn filthy boots off at the freakin' door!!" Now if you would do this for your home why wouldn't you do this for yourself?

101

Amen, brotha! This is a lesson that I am still learning and struggle with-but I have learned that not having boundaries will erode my self-esteem and happiness.

I tried hard at being a nice girl for so long that I had no idea there was another way! A guy would cancel a date with me last minute and I wouldn't say anything. Someone makes a promise and breaks it and nice girl Kim would just say "no problem" and keep quiet. My ex-husband would send a bullying email and I wouldn't respond out of fear of making him more upset. All of these examples are called having no boundaries. Which means anyone in my life could walk all over me and do it over and over and over. They would bring their gross, muddy shoes into my sparkling clean white carpeted house and I would not say a word. Well no more.

Now, if a date cancels last minute for a non-emergency and I politely let him know I deserve more respect and there will be no rain check. A friend or family member breaks a promise, and I let them know I'm disappointed. My ex starts bullying me, and now he knows he will get his ass cussed out. People will think twice about messing with you because they know you will call them on it. So start calling B.S. when appropriate and you will see that necessary boundaries makes for a happier life.

Video: Boundaries and Bullshit
http://www.startdatingagain.net/?page_id=70
Boundaries are enormously important in ALL relationships, even same sex ones. Don't be the nice girl!

Smart is sexy

Do some women really still think that the dumb blonde is something guys desire? Girls that pretend to be what they are not are only considered by men good for one thing, give you one guess what that is. Show off your big brain like you would a bountiful bust! If someone is intimidated, fuck em'! You have just filtered out one more frog. Want to know more? Here is a great story that sends this point home.

Beautiful women and the men tired of f*cking them
by Mike Masters

"What the fuck does she have that I don't?" Like a petulant child she thrust out her ridiculously large breasts and put her hands on her narrow hips. "Are you serious, you want to give up on this??" She motioned with a Vanna White hand towards a body that would capture the eyes of women as strongly as men. Neggy was unbelievably sexy but I would have preferred to force a large grapefruit up my butt than sleep with her again.

"Show me a beautiful woman and I'll show you a man that's tired of fucking her."

I stopped sleeping with knockout Neggy because I met someone that actually stimulated all of me and not just my testicles. Neggy was one of these people that was so attractive that she could rely 100% on the physical, and thus never developed her mental attraction. It disturbed me vastly that I was as drawn to her as a dog would be to sniff another's butt. I internally shook my head, I had to get control over my nuts.

As I wrestled mental control from traitorous fat hairy amigos, I met another girl that opened my understanding. She had a body like a 15 year old boy, wasn't a knockout, was cool/funny as hell and I was stupid attracted to her. Why? Because I needed more sustenance than just dessert, I needed growth and passion, challenge and strife. The new girl was a 7-course feast and Neggy was a punch bowl full of Ben and Jerry's chocolate cookie dough ice cream. (mmmm... makes it almost worth vomiting it back up)

My mind was ecstatically engaged with a woman that pushed and stimulated me, that could fill the sexual glut with mental gymnastics. She created a positive feedback loop that plumped my attraction to her 10 fold that of Neggy-the empty headed narcissist. (Whom I still masturbate over when I don't feel like thinking)

If I look back on the string of women I have dated they usually are not knockouts except in the brains department. In that regard I have insisted on 9's or 10's all of my life. Sure I am like most men, I like a body that I am physically attracted to, but what most people don't understand is that an amazing mind... that I can mental run marathons with... will bump a 6 to an 8... and turn a man viciously protective of that a amazing connection.

104

"Why is it that I am not feeling anything towards him? He is fucking gorgeous, really sweet, an amazing lover, but I want to vomit on his shoes when he tells me he loves me."

Thank God women are wired the same but I think they are willing to put up with the mental inadequacies for eons longer. However, even the strongest female sexual loyalty is inevitably degraded if the gorilla glue of emotional tension does not exist.

"He still makes me laugh and I still annoy the shit out of him." – *my friend Anita on her marriage of 30 years*

They still love each other; you can see it in their eyes and the way they sense the others proximity. They have the tension of the mind, there is struggle, there is massive mutual respect and because their intelligence graces the other, they are less of a person without their partner. A developed mind is the key here, they are both brilliant to the other, they are both intrigued by a brilliance the other respects. They have what all failing relationships lack, a perpetual source of beautiful tension created by the others mind.

Sexual selection Darwin's missing theory

Imagine if the female of a bird species was more sexually attracted to a male with a large colorful tail, now stamp a few million years onto that proclivity. The male's tail would get larger and larger and larger, so ridiculously large that Mindy Mounds would dwindle in comparison. This positive feedback would increase in the bird's tail size indefinitely until it would impair the male's survival against predation or reproduction. (Hint: it's a peacock)

The simple reason why brains are more important than a nice ass

Now what if humans were the same but instead of a tail, men and women sexually selected for intelligence and this positive feed back system blew up our brains (heads) to the point where childbirth threatened both the mother and the fetus. Would that tell you something about humans? Would that tell you something about our sexuality? Would it possibly tell you that if you could put little white panties on our gray matter it would be hands-down the sexiest organ one could ever possess?

105

Sexual selection is a Darwinian theory that is ignored by all textbooks simply because it was not mathematically provable until recently. We might seem like physical creatures to you but the flashiest, sexiest part of our anatomy is that squishy jello mold in your noggin. If you are not using it to its fullest capacity in your attempts to attract the opposite sex you might as well be Cinderella wearing a potato sac to the ball.

This appears to not be the case since we are biased by the fact initial attraction is very much physical and we give it WAY too much weight. The mental is really where that concrete relationship is developed and cemented, not in the fleeting physical.

You spend time at the gym, you spend time on your hair but do you spend time making your mind more attractive?

Preparation Bullets:

I believe part two, preparation is the most important section of the book, and is where most of us are weakest. Please take the time to really internalize these concepts, if need be repeat this chapter a couple of times. There is a lot of tough stuff here and if you miss it, you will flounder with frustration in the dating world.

- I think you are already aware of who the losers and winners are, but sometimes we need a little reminding, especially if we keep dating the losers!
- If you find yourself repeating patterns, you need to reprogram. This is done by spotlighting pleasure and reinforcing pain, these are wonderful tools that can be applied to all negative patterns.
- Understanding yourself is the first step in understanding who is well matched for you. Are you Fire? Water? Creative? Or Logical?
- Your match is your opposite. Dating yourself not only is boring but often you will learn to hate your partner for having all the same negative traits you do.
- Sexual tension is probably the least understood concept in attraction, memorize how it works, and you suddenly will have total control.
- Sexual tension cannot last without a balance of power. Are you calling too much? You are giving away power. Jealous? Giving away power. STOP IT!! REMEMBER THE TEETER TOTTER!
- Remember this quote? "Most importantly, they need some space to realize that they miss us." Tattoo this to the inside of your forehead.

- You can't hit a target you can't see, define your target first and then take some practice shots, and don't give up. Every master once sucked, even Bruce Lee.
- Set up your target but realize that your target is moving. Demanding a certain outcome is counter productive and will give you a tumor. Rather, say to yourself, "This would be nice," and let go.
- Setting intention is not the "law" of attraction, rather there is no law, if there were we would have no struggles and life would be quite dull. Setting intension is something different, it is laying out a request, if it is something "life" feels is beneficial to you, it will manifest.
- Without confidence there is no action and without action there is no result. So: Fake it until you make it, just do it, confidence is key, feel the fear and do it anyway. You get this right?
- Being sexy is first loving you, feeling the sexiness from inside. Don't feel this? Take the actions needed to fix this, it is not as far away as you think.
- Don't get hung up on "the game" sure it would be nice to not have to play but It would make attraction rather dull. Understand that the game is played unconsciously and if you don't play, you lose.

Actions:

This chapter is not very action oriented because it is preparing you to get back out there. True action will be in the next chapter, so with that said, did you make the lists like we asked? If not, how can you expect yourself to act on something far more challenging? Finish the list, set your intention, and get ready to aim at that target a few times.

1. Obviously if you haven't done it go back and make your lists of who you want and who you don't want. Type up the Who I want list, print it, and tape it to your bathroom mirror. (Make sure to hide it if he comes for a visit)
2. Do you know who you are? Are you a Lover? A Queen? Who is your opposite? Can you place friends in some of these Archetypes? Can you relate some killer relationships to the fact that you were opposites? Practice this, and then wow your friends by predicting their relationship failure or success.
3. Start being aware of power balance all around you. Are dogs more aggressive with you because you are afraid of them? Are men fearful of you because you are aggressive? Are you treated poorly at work by someone with more power? Do you treat someone else poorly because you have more power? Once you are aware of this, see if you can manipulate that power. Say "NO" more often to gain power or give your power away to someone weak.
4. Take stock of your internal state, do you feel sexy? If not time to do something about it NOW, set an intention (goal) and write down the 10 most effective things you could do to get to that goal. Aside: As a nutritionist everyone asks me what is the most important thing they can change to lose weight. I always say the same thing, "accountability". Want to make a change? Be

accountable to someone. Here is an old blog post I wrote on this concept http://fulltimevagabond.com/2009/10/03/the-magic-of-getting-things-done-through-a-little-destruction/

5. Start reprogramming: If some of the concepts in this chapter hit you, it is imperative to stamp them to your brain. I want you to put up reminders of this information around your home. For example, buy a white board marker and write on your bathroom mirror, "I allow men the time to miss me" or maybe in permanent marker you write on the inside of your underwear, "You NEVER come off on the first date." Hahaha, I like that one. The brain is highly reluctant to change and you must use any tool you can to remove negative patterns and create positive ones.

6. Resistant to the game? Well before you throw the baby out with the bathwater add a really fascinating book to your reading list. It is called Ignore and Score and was written by a good friend of mine. The book is written for men but it doesn't matter, all the same concepts apply in the opposite direction. Robby breaks down the game beautifully and I honestly wish I wrote his book. http://www.amazon.com/How-Get-Girl-Explained-ebook/dp/B004MDLSBQ (Not an affiliate link)

Part three: Execution

Since you have been out of the game for while this might be the most baffling part about the whole process. Where the hell are guys??? So before you hit your local bar and hook up with a guy that just won the local title for belching, let's think about this for a second.

First, what do you want? We talked about this a ton earlier so hopefully this is clear now. You might have the perfect man in mind, but without a little ACTION nothing will happen. Unless the UPS or pizza/delivery guys are your type, because they're the only men who are going to knock on your door.

I have already said that finding the perfect guy is going to take a little while. I cannot show you the target, give a bow and arrow and expect you to hit the bulls-eye in the first go. So... maybe it is time for a little practice shooting? Maybe you would consider a little recreational dating?

IX. Dating again

Recreational dating

I have a friend of mine named Victoria, she is 35 and been divorced for over a year. Victoria was married for 8 years before she finally left the guy she was married to. This was hard for her because along with leaving a very wealthy man she had three daughters. Victoria amazingly, started her own business distributing healthy food vending machines around southern California. This gave her the independence to take care of herself and her daughters.

Why do I bring Victoria up? I met Victoria at a club while she was grinding on a ripped younger guy. She was having a great time, resetting her life and reliving her 20's. She was acting very similar to the way she was before she got married. She was having fun dating a bit and having some frivolous sex along the way.

I might be biased because I really enjoy frivolous sex but I think it is very important to get back out in the mix and tramp around a bit. Why? I feel that it helps women regain their sexuality; it helps them get back into the mix very similar to the stage she was in before she was married in the first place.

If you find yourself in the role of the cougar, you might really enjoy the story below. I adore the cougar and I want there to be a ton more of her kind.

Cougar, cutting her claws on the back of change
By Mike Masters

Demi Moore married actor Ashton Kucher when she was 42 and he was 27. Madonna, now 50-years-old is dating Brazilian model Jesus Luz, only 22.

Bar fly

"They work out like I do. Guys my age are fat and gross. I want the total package. I deserve the total package. I want hot and funny."
This is what society handed me," said Spuehler, chatting on a recent Thursday night. "I thought when I was in my 20s, I would find somebody and have a beautiful life with him and have children." Exit the husband. Enter the fawning young men. – Denver Post

She doesn't need you

I have sat on the topic of cougars for a long time, simply because there seemed to be something moving in the background of deeper understanding. There appeared to be more and all I was seeing was the fin above the surface, not the shark creating it.

Recently and for reasons I still don't understand, I have been meeting and talking to quite a few women who are older than me, very fit, financially independent, and extremely intelligent. I was sure this type of woman was new, I had been out of the states for over 8 years, and the gradual warming of the pot didn't blind me to such changes like it did for most men.

I stuck my tongue into my cheek and thought, something is odd here, where did all these older powerful sexy women come from? and the term cougar?? I hadn't heard it before I left the states 8 years earlier. Why is it so common now? Is something changing in the US, and possibly around the world?

Above are some interesting indicators of change: Demigoddesses of Hollywood are fearlessly displaying younger men. Your local bar has a few new members, unabashed about what they want. These signs appear insignificant but I am convinced they represent something much larger.

While talking to a writer friend yesterday, we hit upon something that we couldn't see independently. (She of course is single, fit, beautiful, intelligent and ten years older than I am) "I know what you mean, something deeper is happening here." We continued to explore until we excitingly struck some pay dirt.

Wanna know what it is? Women are making more money, they are getting divorced sooner (because they CAN), they are fit and body conscious, they look younger, they are powerful, and they feel less and less tethered to men. To put it simply, the 30+ year old woman NO LONGER FEELS SHE NEEDS A MAN.

Now some of you might be thinking, "That is no revelation because I don't need a man either," (add pissy head wobble) could women honestly say this 10 years ago? 20? I would argue that this has snuck up on the western world and its implications are much larger than you can imagine. I believe this is the second stage of the feminist movement; this is the seizing of real power by millions and millions of successful women. This is a leveling of the playing field that we have only been seeing in the last ten years. AND it is potentially very terrifying or incredibly exciting for millions and millions of men.

The younger man

When I was a competitive swimmer in high school we delightfully trained coed. Interestingly, in the water women are nearly physically equivalent to men and often faster in long distance. So, I shouldn't have been so upset when a new girl was a stronger swimmer than I. If it were a guy, my tender young ego would only be bruised, but a girl? This was too much for me since it not only threatened my ego but my masculinity.

I believe this is why we have derogatory terms like cougar. I believe it is a name slapped on older, successful women to degrade their success and protect male masculinity. The fat man in the Lexus is a far more common dinosaur than its freshly evolved equivalent: the mature sexy woman in the convertible mini cooper. This leaves the fit older woman severely lacking her equal, a fit man, at her success level that isn't threatened by her new status. What does that leave her with?

The younger man isn't upset that she drives a better car, has a better job, or wants to fuck him better than he has ever been fucked. He looks at this type of woman with stars in his eyes and wood in his pants. She looks at him for what he is, fun, fit, carefree and with a penis that doesn't need to

114

be fueled by Viagra and a shot of whiskey. After all she just got out of a 15 year marriage and she is entering her second 20's but separate from her 25 year-old prey she is doing it with confidence and a bit o' cash. She is going to really savor it this time around and AMEN, She deserves it.

Where is this going?

I think it was a wonderful thing when my female nemesis joined the swim team, my initial reaction was poor but soon enough I had to raise my own game. I trained harder got faster and developed a crazy attraction to this girl. I became better because of her, but cultural standards of sexual inequality made me initially bitter. I think this is what this second feminist movement is about to face, a confused angry resistance to their success. A childlike lashing out against their new found power. Powerful single women over thirty need to be prepared for this masculine insecurity, younger women need to be aware of the ring they are about to enter.

Make no mistake, power is transferring and just like the US bitching and moaning about China, most men won't see this as a positive. This is where the new woman needs to hold her ground and weather the inevitable storm. She needs to let the term cougar be one of power, ignoring the blatherings of the fat man stuck in his Lexus. She needs to embrace that she is the vehicle of change not only for her daughters but for her sons that eventually will have to step up to the plate and embrace this new woman.

I adore the new cougar and I want nothing more than to watch her cut her claws on the back of change.

Getting yourself back in the groove

A good friend of mine is trying to recreational date but she is screwing it up royally. Why? Because she is desperate for two things: sexual intimacy and a serious relationship. This means that every guy she meets she has sex with way too soon and then piles on relationship expectation so thick, that all of them run screaming. I want you to get back out there but I don't want you to follow in my friend's tracks. I hate the fact that she is starting to feel bitter towards men due to something she is creating.

115

No expectations

Getting back in the groove means getting back in the mix without, I repeat, WITHOUT any expectations. It is very important for you to get into the mindset of an attractive, independent woman that does not need a man. Sure, you can think about how nice it would be but the second you put that need out there is the second you repel men.

It is necessary to regain that frivolous fun attitude you had in college, regain the girl that didn't need anyone but her friends and family. The sooner you become this person the more attractive you will become to men.

Fishing for the big one

Most fisherman that are any good at what they do put out multiple lines. This radically raises their chances of catching the kind of fish they want. However, it also does something that you wouldn't expect.

Imagine a fisherman that only puts out one line. He cast out the line than he stared at it, jiggled it a bit, reeled it in and jiggled it again. For some reason beyond his comprehension the fish hit the bait but never took the hook. One day the fisherman got a little frustrated with having only one line in the water and he threw out two more and opened a beer and relaxed. The pull of one of the lines snapped him out of sleep and he jumped. To his amazement all three lines had fish on them! "Why," he asked himself? I gave no attention to those lines, could it be why the fish were skittish, because of my need? Wow... he thought I should not care more often!! And he did, eventually catching the trophy fish.

I tell men and women this constantly and I think there is no better time to practice it than now. Go out with a few people, keep yourself busy with multiple dates, lay back have a beer and don't give a shit! Possibly to your shock (but not mine) the increased interest guys show will blow your mind. Remember, there is nothing more attractive than the unobtainable/unavailable.

So the goal is to get back out there, with the trophy fish in mind but zero expectation of landing him initially. I don't want you to even look for him! Just get out there and try your hand. This is part of the process and must occur before you will find that one amazing guy. The sooner you get proficient at this, is the sooner you will be able to meet someone that really matters.

A Grown Ass Woman's Perspective on Recreational Dating

Kim Hess Divorce Guru has many opinions on recreational dating. My first opinion being that a woman can only truly date recreationally before they hit the age of 25. After the age of 25 some magic switch is pulled and we ladies start looking for a man. Not just any man, but a man who we can one day call "my man". Even if you just got rid of one husband or boyfriend and have sworn off marriage/commitment and its trappings for life, when you start dating again that will all quickly fly out the window.

Now honestly, being a happily divorced woman, I cannot sit here (or stand, or recline) and tell you that when I date a guy I'm not thinking of what he will be like long term...long term as in marriage. Scary isn't it? I have no intention or desire of being anyone's wife but to even consider dating a guy more than a few months (okay, you got me, a few weeks, weeks!) he would have to be ~~good~~ great long-term relationship material. Hence, the reason I've had lots of dates but no long-term relationships since my divorce!

That said, I'm a bit biased when people (Mike) suggests to me or any other woman who has loved then lost, that we should just slut around. I get the rationale. Any psychologist, relationship coach, or tarot card reader will tell a woman who's just got out of a deep, loving, committed, devoted relationship not to jump into another relationship. To "just have fun" and "play the field." Or as my co-author says to just "slut around!"

But as much as I hate to admit…they're all right.

Pros of Casual Dating

I have a very good female friend named Joanna; she is a petite red head that loves to screw. She has taken me home and my best friend; she is also being hunted or is hunting most of the guys in the area. She loves sex, she loves having fun and if a guy tries to commit to her she bails. Guys are insane over her, they send her flowers, they buy her dinner, they stalk her, fall instantly in love, and last but not least, beg her for commitment. What is going on here?

This is so simple, Joanna is simply taking on the male role, and in response, the guys are taking on the female. Does she want a great guy? Yes. Is she a bit different to be so sexually brazen/cold? Yeah, too bad I can't bottle it. Has "slutting around" made her incredibly successful and attractive to men? Hell yeah!

You might want to consider becoming a Hoe-a-saurs for a short time, it might be fun, and it might teach you a ton about men and sex.

I've done this. I've honestly tried to be a slut…that is having casual, fun sex, or casual fun dates with no strings attached as far as exclusivity or long term plans. Yeah, it's fun. The good times without the bad. The fun being the new sex partner, the nights out, the bottles of wine, the sexy text messages, the great dinners, the excitement of learning about someone new. Not having to put up with his mother who thinks you're not good enough for her pookey-wookems, no pouring a bowl of cereal only to find an empty carton of milk, no putting up with his boring co-workers at their lame birthday parties. Not being married or in a committed relationship means you don't have to deal with the bad. And you can eat cookies in bed with your clay facemask on watching a Lifetime for Women movie marathon. So far so good.

Cons of Casual Dating

Until your birthday. Or wanting to get away with someone for the weekend which is a definite no-no if you're just slutting around. Or Valentine's Day comes and he's "busy." No explanation, just busy. Which he has every right to be since you both are just having fun. Because while he's having fun, every time you have sex with him you get more and more emotionally bonded.

Women are programmed to date for relationships, commitment. Men are programmed to date for sex, for fun. I'm not saying that women can't date for fun or great sex. We may start out with that intention in mind. But then we start to like the guy. A lot. Because of the fun we're having with him, we want more. As much as possible. And we want that fun to be just for us, not for other women he may be (and probably is) dating. Same with sex. If the sex is good we want more. If the sex is great we want to own the man that's giving us this great sex. And how do women think they own someone? Commitment. Men can have great fun with a woman and great sex and never feel they

119

must snag her into a relationship right away. Men tend to fall in love slowly. Us ladies? We're planning the honeymoon and wondering when we should take him home to meet the parents after our first phone conversation!

I totally agree with what Kim is saying here since I have to constantly be on alert with any woman I am dating (sleeping with). Chances are she, like Kim said, is planning our honeymoon. What I will argue with is, that if you can execute (as in murder) the ludicrous thoughts of commitment, you will find men acting in ways you have never seen before.

Girl, Let's Be Honest

Here are a few things I want you to ask yourself about whether or not to casually engage in sexual relations:

Are you being honest about what you really want? Have you sat down, in silence, and gotten honest with the wonderful woman you call you? I must admit to you, my fellow "broken hearted-but stayin' strong" ladies: I went through a time where I SAID I wanted casual no strings attached sex. I SAID I didn't need a man for nothin' but sex, and I was happy living my life with flings, one night stands, and having a plethora of men in and out of my social life. But then I realized I wasn't having all that much fun and got real with myself.

I admitted that I really wanted companionship, love, and a man I could connect with more ways than just sex. Once I was honest with Kim Hess Divorce Guru I realized that casual sex wasn't going to make me feel better. (Well, it did make me feel better -a lot better- but only for a few hours. Oh, okay, sometimes days!) After that I would feel sad and lonely knowing that I had just had sex with someone who could care less about me. Is this okay with you? If it is, go for it, keep your head up, and always bring your own condoms. If you really want a loving caring relationship, be honest with yourself...sex without commitment is probably not for you.

Do you value who you are no matter what anyone else thinks of you? Casual sex shouldn't be a venue to validate how wanted or sexy you are...you should already be validated and know that you are all that!

You've also got to be comfortable and know that there is a possibility of rejection. If you are having great casual sex with someone, know that there is a big possibility that it may come to an end. That fun, exciting one night stand may be busy when you call him back for another fun exciting one night stand. The guy who you're having consistent awesome sex with (you've heard the term "Friends With Benefits"?) might decide to have awesome consistent sex with someone else. Or heaven forbid he decide to have an awesome consistent relationship with someone else! Are you going to be able to handle that? Your brain may say yes but will your heart? Can you stay in the moment of great sex or will you take it home with you? Ruminating that he would be the perfect boyfriend because he's a doctor and surfs? Will your self-esteem suddenly come to a screeching halt leaving you on your sofa with big fat tears dripping into your ice cream? (Uh, once again, divas, my real experience!)

The shoe could possibly be on the other foot if you're using someone for a good time and they decide they want more. If you don't want more are you going to have the ability to hightail it out of the relationship to save his feelings and avoid any upcoming drama? If the answer is no, avoid the sex.

It's Raining Men: Got Your Rubbers?

With casual sex comes being committed to protection. After being married or in a long term relationship, sexual history and monogamy was probably discussed and the protection discarded. Not so with casual relationships. Are you okay with having protected sex? You know, condoms EVERY time you have sex not just most of the time? Do you have protection against unwanted pregnancies? My ex had a vasectomy so I was totally off the hook with the possibility of getting pregnant. Not so now because that little (big) detail is now up to me! (Damn, if only all men I slept with could get fixed!)

What does casual sex mean to you? Seeing each other only when it comes to sexy time? Is dinner and a movie before hot sex considered casual to you, but relationship to your sex partner? Decide now before your heart gets broken when you want to order take out Chinese and watch HBO with your casual sex partner and he wants nothing but you on a silver platter. In other words, make sure that your expectations are equal and avoid easily avoidable misunderstandings.

Okay, because Kim is not around, I can slip in one more argument without her responding. (Hahaha!)

Negative emotions can be controlled, shifted and turned into something quite positive. The reason Kim and many other women feel that "slutting around" is so negative, is because they have relationship expectation. Yes, women produce a ton of hormones from sex that scream to their subconscious, "Keep him! Own him! He is mine and only mine! Him being with another means less for me!" This chatter is untrue; it is stemmed from a belief that love, passion, and connection can only be had with one. Love is like air, there is no limit to it, and trying to keep a man after intimacy only means you think another woman breathing the same air means less for you.

122

Right now, behind me, my girlfriend is talking, flirting and having fun with another man. Am I jealous? Yes, and no. I do not own her, and her having fun with another guy does not take away from me. Yes this is a very difficult concept, but one I hope you can challenge in your life. When you can let go, and see that love, sex, and intimacy can be shared, you will suddenly receive so much more of it.

I hope you take the time to learn more about this, read the book Ethical Slut if you feel you are ready to expand your mind into this challenging paradigm.
http://www.amazon.com/Ethical-Slut-Infinite-Sexual-Possibilities/dp/1890159018

X. The where - Dating logistics

I know you're wondering, "Where do I, a fabulous and lovely woman, find a man who is worthy? Or do I let him find me? Or do I hope that one day we will mutually look into each other's eyes and realize we cannot live without one another?" Well that's a question for the ages. Fortunately, we've got the answers!

It's Raining Men

Men are everywhere. Yes, I said everywhere! All you have to do is walk outside and you will see a plethora of the opposite sex swarming your path. They are at church, hardware stores, restaurants, running marathons, at your work place, on the elevator, your neighbors, your kid's school teachers, the plumber…the list goes on and on. Now comes the hard part. Weeding out the men you could actually be interested in! Oh, and you know that hot guy you exchanged smiles with while getting your triple shot no-foam latte? He's gay.

So I know this is a little obvious right? But is it? I think that after a devastating separation the place we want to be is home alone not out and about! But this is where the men are! They are out there, and there are literally thousands and thousands of them that are totally compatible with you. So the question is are you going to sit on your ass with a bowl of Ben and Jerry's or are you going to find him before some other sexy woman swipes him??

Hey I know it is a little intimidating for you to run out and sign up with your local church to feed the homeless, just so that you can land Mr. Perfect. If you find this somewhat daunting maybe you should ease back into the game with a little online dating first?

Looking by looking – is online dating for you?

I am a hands-on person; I like to personally interact with someone before any date action occurs. However, just because online dating is not my forte does not mean it is not valid. A friend of mine lives in the middle of nowhere and relies solely on three dating sites for the guys in her life. She gets lots of dates on a regular basis.

Internet dating is definitely something that is growing rapidly and will only get better as time goes on. If this you want to cut to the chase and kiss a bunch of frogs this might be the way to go.

Okay did I just say that Internet dating is growing rapidly??? STRIKE THAT, it is fricken' growing out of control! 40 million users in the US are using online dating? Holy trannys on unicycles Batman! Considering the population of the US is currently around 300 million what does that tell you??? That means that over 13% of the US population is looking for love. Wow...

Just like that little black dress

The easiest way to find these men in my opinion is online dating. It's like shopping for that cute black cocktail dress that is timeless. The only problem with that perfect little black dress is trying on a lot of other not so perfect dresses to get to the one.

You have to approach finding a man online like you would finding that awesome little black dress online. I understand that it's not quite the same but it is a surprisingly similar process. While shopping for a dress you need to know your size, what price range you're looking for, and if you're in the market for a short revealing dress or ankle length ball gown.

Same with looking for a date online. Where do you want to look for this guy: 10 miles from where you live or maybe from the other side of the world? Do you go search for the extroverted, charismatic guys who in their profile talk about surfing and skydiving or do you gravitate towards the bookish geeks who wax poetically about Shakespeare and stay in Friday nights drinking excellent bourbon? Your pick, just like the dress.

Just as you put all your criteria in for the dress you're hoping to buy, you put in all the criteria for the man you're hoping to date. The results? Sometimes hopeful, sometimes disappointing. All the dresses may be ugly. So are the men. A few of the dresses may be perfect, but too expensive: some of the men you may be attracted to may not be attracted to you or live in France and you live in Ohio. Maybe the dress you like is the right style but they don't have your size: he's an atheist and you are a very devout Catholic.

So what do you do? You search, you sift through, you broaden or change what you're looking for. Instead of a dress that's 100% silk (Doctor), you may relax your standards a little for a great dress that's a silk/rayon blend (hot construction worker). Instead of wanting a similar dress you saw Angelina Jolie wear to the Oscars (Brad Pitt), you may settle on a pretty good substitution for you to wear to your cousin Amy's wedding (Vince Vaughn).

And don't forget that just as there are many, many websites to find little black dresses, there are many, many sites to find a great date. Casual dresses, casual dating…I'd suggest Plenty of

Fish. It's free, and because it's free men may not be the highest quality or going to last long…kind of like a cheap dress. It's cute, and trendy but after you wash it a few times it loses its cuteness! Looking for something more long term, one of those dresses that you still wear after 5 years that's classic and great quality? That I would suggest a site like E-Harmony, Match.com or a similar paid site. You pay good money, and there is quality control testing in the form of a gazillion questions before they find you a man. I could go on and on. Want a sleazy dress that will get you lots of looks and sex…Craigslist.org. Need help paying the rent or getting pretty jewelry? That would be the little black dress you wouldn't necessarily wear to church on Sunday morning-AshleyMadison.com or a Sugar Daddy site. The list is virtually (get it virtual, virtually?) endless.

Keep in mind what you do want in that perfect little black dress, and more importantly what you DON'T want! Same goes for the men that you date.

All in all, online dating is fun and sometimes an ego boost. It can also crush you like an ant and have you wondering if you will ever find a nice guy to date. These times come up when you write the "perfect guy" and you never hear back from him. Or you email a guy back and forth for weeks, never to have him ask you to meet in person or declining your invitations for a face-to-face date.

Online dating can be yucky too ☹

There are also icky moments when you get a man 30 years older than you writing to you about leather, and sex, and bondage. Yeah, it happens (I still shudder at the thought!) Or when men with weird or gross screen names write you: "blackmeatbythepound" or "ihatemyxgf" or "oral4u69". Yeah, I don't have to tell you to stay away from these online daters!

127

(blackmeatbythepound was me actually. Hey! I might be white but I am black where it counts!)

Shopping online is fun and convenient and you can do it in your pajamas without the mall crowds. But when all is said and done, all of the best little black dresses that I've purchased and loved the best, came from actually getting my broken hearted butt off the couch and leaving my house to shop. I could make sure it fit just right, and could feel the material, and properly assess the quality before buying. Just like a potential date. In other words, get OFFline.

Wounded Bird Syndrome – Online predation
By Kim Hess and Mike Masters

I was getting lots of attention from less than desirable men.

These men included:

25 year olds that would write to me asking if I wanted to hang out (have sex)
55 year olds asking if I would like to get together for some adult fun (have sex)
35-45 year olds (my desired age range) asking if I wanted to have a friends with benefits relationship (have sex)

I asked Mike what was going on in the minds of all these men that would have them bring up sex right away. He grinned through the phone, and told me this is what he calls, "Wounded Bird Syndrome." This is what Mike helped me understand about this type of guy.

When a bird is wounded and can't fly, predators (think cats) immediately sense their inability to escape and then eat their ass.

Now let's translate this: Women, after a devastating break up or divorce, are damaged. Some men can sense this and these men will use this to their advantage to get what they want...quick and easy sex from a lonely needy woman new to the dating scene.

The majority of women turn to online dating looking for love. A large number of men go online looking for sex. Unfortunately there is a large group of men who get high success by dating online and benefiting from the "Wounded Bird Syndrome."

Statistics show that 1 out of 3 women who meet men online have sex the first time they meet, of those women 4 out of 5 didn't use protection! (Huffington Post.com via Online Schools March 25,2010)

I believe some men see that my profile includes divorcee, and children and assume I'm a wounded bird or an easy target. Some of those men were right. Once upon a time I was bored, lonely, and newly single. I was too emotionally worn out to pick myself up off the couch and socialize to meet new friends and lovers. So I dated online. My radar for knowing a good guy from a bad guy was way off. I was one of those

129

desperate online daters and I was easy prey for men whose only goal was to date me for sex.

Who's more likely to be online? Active fun people with lots of friends, activities, and a full and fun life? Or those who are too scared to go out and experience life? A lot of people date online because they can stay home where it's safe and easy.

I'm not proclaiming that all people online are boring and desperate or dating online is horrible and you won't meet anyone who is in it for a long term relationship. I'm just warning you, from my own experience, that you must go out and interact in person. You can only gather a certain amount of information about someone who you have never met in real life.

When we meet someone in person we can gather millions of bits of information: Their body language, how they smell, how they interact, their physical presence, and the list goes on and on. Pictures can lie, and you can never be truly attracted to someone until you are face to face with them.

Online dating is still relatively new and has some maturing to do. Until it gets to the point of being full-grown, I urge you to take precaution if you're still a little beat up from your old relationship. It's okay to be a wounded bird, just don't become the online prey of that one guy out of a hundred that knows how to feed on your weakness.

So Where the Offline Is He?

This is probably the most crucial part, finding that great guy and getting back out there. You know what you want, you know what you don't want, but getting back out there actually involves some ACTION!

Taking action to make it happen!

You can have the greatest intentions in the world but without action very little will ever happen. Sure, it is frightening to get back out there, to walk into a club where you are the oldest one there, to flirt with a guy in the grocery store only to see a ring on his finger, to ask out a coworker and find out later he is gay. Change is intimidating, but it is really really important to reframe this feeling. Change CAN be intimidating but it also can be really wonderful and exciting! You have just changed ships and are now on a completely different journey. Don't hide in your cabin waiting for the voyage to be over, rather embrace it and have a kick ass time!

Increase your social circle

To get back out there we first need to push some comfort zones. I imagine that your current social circle is pretty small, everybody knows everybody and all the guys are probably married or in a relationship (and you need some fresh meat to cut your teeth on!) So in order to meet someone new you must expand your social circle or die trying. What does this mean? You must make some pretty big changes! Really want it to happen fast? Move to a new city and you will meet, and have the desire to meet, a ton of new people. So let's say you don't want to move to a new city or change your job. What can you do right now, tomorrow or next week to meet more people?

My secret to finding dates: Looking by not looking

I have been constantly amazed at where and how I have met wonderful people:

- Took a salsa class and dated my instructors (just kidding with the plural)
- Met a GORGEOUS older woman while teaching a nutrition class

- While throwing a party for a good friend of mine the most amazing woman came, I immediately fell in love
- Met my longest relationship at a wedding I was the minister of
- Fell in love with a Thai stewardess I met while traveling in Bangkok
- Dated and had the serious hots for my professor when studying Japanese
- Met the sexiest girl of my life while dancing in a club in Tokyo (took a day trip there)
- While running a marathon I ran the last 5 miles with a girl I later dated
- Got a random New Years kiss from the younger sister of a new friend while visiting New York
- While experimenting with online dating I actually met someone pretty cool on Plenty of Fish
- Experienced a WONDERFUL one night relationship with a French girl while bicycling across the US

Do you recognize the key here? Each time I was not actively looking but I was active, doing something new, meeting new people, trying new things. How in the world can you meet someone great when you are not meeting anyone new!?

Kill your damn TV

I live what I teach, and getting out there is something you must do, and it can be a wonderful, wonderful experience. Part of the reason I meet so many people is because I am constantly doing new things and meeting new people. My design is not to meet people but to have a good time and learn something new. This makes it all the more authentic when meeting someone interesting. Meeting someone new is not my agenda; I am there for something else (ironically even my experience on the dating site Plenty Of Fish was like this; not interested in meeting anyone just wanted to understand online dating more.)

Good men are everywhere

A lot of people will tell you that to find a good guy you need to be in good places, like church or volunteer work. This is a bunch of malarkey! (Is that still a word??)

Good people are everywhere. Good people go to bars, churches, AA meetings, and the gym. The secret is to get out there, to raise your energy, to get back into the pipeline, and meet some kick ass people!

Okay… I still don't get it, where do I meet good people?

My point is to look for a new person by not looking; this is the most sincere and most effective way to find someone. It is also one of the best ways to really increase happiness in your life. Getting out there and learning, doing, becoming someone new is enormous. Not only does this put you in a happier place but it makes you a more attractive person. When you bump into that guy that you thought was pretty cool, you are going to have the aura of someone growing, someone excited about life. This is a huge turn on and will draw men to you like flies to shit, or better yet like fudge on ice cream? Did I ruin that analogy?

Mike, you're so gross!

But I don't have TIME!

You may be thinking: "I don't have TIME to meet new people or do new things, can't I just meet someone online?!

BullShit... Time is very much a condition of priorities and bad habits. I once dropped everything, sold everything, quit everything for a 3 month bicycle ride across the US and Canada. Suddenly, I had all the time in the world! This was shear bliss, one of the greatest experiences of my life.

You might be saying "But I can't do that, I have kids!?" Come on... I saw a family of 5 on two tandem bicycles with a kid's seat on the back of one, wow!
I even know a family of four currently sailing around the world... with no TV! So you don't have time??? Why don't you rephrase this to be a little more accurate?

"I am too afraid to change my life, so it appears like I don't have time."

Okay, that is more like it.

So am I asking you to upend your life? Sure! If you want to! But it isn't necessary; I just want you to make room for a few more activities a week. Activities that you really want to learn and will help introduce you to new social circles.

Create a quick list to help yourself out

What are some of the things I would love to do/learn to expand my social circle?

1. Join a morning boot camp
2. Learn Yoga
3. Study French and stay in France for one month
4. Start my own internet business selling jewelry (I have met a TON of people from my online business)
5. For lunch, eat at a new restaurant once a week
6. Go to a speed dating event with a friend, just for fun
7. Take a Thai cooking class
8. Try sky diving with my best guy friend
9. Study...
10. Visit...
11. Try...
12. Live in...
13. Love...
14. Dance...
15. Create...

These are high-energy activities that get you into the mix again. They are not intentionally designed for finding a guy but regardless they will work. Even if your Thai cooking class is full of women it doesn't matter, it is very probable that through your new social circle you will meet that incredible guy. Plus, women that know you are single and looking will be on the lookout for a compatible guy for you. This is such a win/win and it totally takes away the needy "I need to find a guy" attitude you might be emanating.

I know it's hard but you gotta do it!

I relied on online dating for a long time. Why? Because I was hiding. Hiding from the outside world and wallowing in my own sadness about being divorced. I didn't get out there because I was afraid of the outside world. I want you to ask yourself why you are afraid? What's holding you back from experiencing life and having a great time?

I swore off online dating for a period of months, in an attempt to force myself out of my online fantasy world and into the real world with real people. I found that just being out and about that I met people. I accepted every invitation that came my way. I started asking friends I haven't seen in awhile if they wanted to hang out. I began going out by myself, just to get out of the house. I went on a particularly bad date (the guy had greased back hair and yellow teeth) and instead of being discouraged and going home to sulk, I took myself dancing. Yes, I went to a club by myself and got my groove on! Yes, it was scary, but after 30 minutes I realized it was totally worth overcoming the fear. I had 3 men ask me for my number that night... one from the club and two as I was walking home. I took a chance and had a great time and met new men. This would not have happened if I were solely dating online.

I believe online dating can be great because you meet people you wouldn't normally interact with. But also believe dating online can lead to isolation and comfort, neither one of those is gonna get you what you want.

XI. Dating has changed and hasn't - Technology

What's changed?

All the fundamental rules of dating are the same, whether or not you are in the 1950's or are in a different culture. This means that riding the proverbial dating bicycle again will be intuitive. Don't be one of the people that tell themselves, "How can I get back into things again? I haven't dated in 10 years! And with this new fangled Internet to boot! What the heck do I do?"

The above dating bicycle analogy is very appropriate, you knew how to do it once and getting back on might be a tad scary but it will also be exciting and come back to you a lot faster than you think. Not only that but with my help we can get you better at riding that bike than you ever were in the past!

With that said there are a few things that are a bit different on this current bike everyone rides but it is not very daunting. Trust me, and hang on!

The New Way

What has changed with dating is probably something that you already use but maybe not in a dating sense. The use of technology to connect with the opposite sex, Facebook, Twitter, Match.com even Skype are now dating tools for young and old. Don't want to be confused as hell when he asks you to Skype chat with him? Than read on so you won't feel like a dingus.

When to use online dating

I know you're thinking: "Wasn't this already covered? Online dating is such a huge part of the dating world that we couldn't possibly cover it in ten sections let along two.

A lot of people have embraced online dating and some with a lot of success. Is online dating for you? I think it has its place for quite a few people with certain conditions

- You are older and it is very hard to meet men your age – I used to work for a 70-year-old woman that met tons of men online. When I asked her why she did this she replied, "There are very few men my age out there and meeting new people gets more and more difficult every year, all the eligible men keep dying!" Is she right? Yeah the crowd does thin a bit with age, especially if your date might have a heart attack with his next orgasm. Amazingly, she runs into many of the same problems most women that date online do. "Most of the guys out there are just interested in sex," she said as she hefted her large bosom towards me. Eeewww...

- You live in the middle of nowhere and networking is hell – Another friend of mine says she is forced to date online because she lives 40 miles from any large city. This is a very valid reason for using online dating. Unfortunately, because she doesn't have a lot of time she accepts full dates the first time meeting (as opposed to the mini date we explain later on). A big mistake which has gotten her: a lot of one night stands, creepy dudes that stalk her, angry wives that call her, and general chaos.

- You are super duper busy and don't have time – Two of my friends got married after meeting on match.com. Why did they use it? Because they were both so consumed with their careers that networking was something they felt they couldn't do. It worked for them, but now they hate each other. ☺

- You like the sheer numbers of people you can meet – When I arrived in a small town in northern Michigan I was amazed at how many people I found in the middle of nowhere! I met about 2 people a day online (granted half of them had 15 kids and worked at McDonalds). I never would have met as many people even if I went out to the bars every night.

- You are really really shy and like the "shield" that being online gives – It might be far less intimidating to you than going to a speed dating event. In a few senses this is very true, getting back on the bike means getting back into the mindset of dating again. Online dating can be like training wheels. You are shielded online and you can flirt, joke and practice without having the stress of talking face to face.

- You think that online engines are better at weeding out the garbage – They might be but I have not seen any proof to this yet and personally I think their matching systems are a bunch of BULL…

Gee, do I sound biased? But once again I am not an expert at online dating and I suggest further research if you are bound and determined to go this route.

I **am** an expert at online dating and want to tell you if you must, must, MUST date online, put your best foot forward! On my radio show Divorce Guru I interviewed an Online Dating Expert. Listen to file://localhost/c:/Users/Kim%20Hess/Downloads/.%20(http:/www.energytalkradio.com/programsshows.html&show=13&recording=218 here with Laurie Davis, eFlirt Expert who's also been interviewed by ABC World News, Health, and NPR to give her opinion on how to online date effectively. Don't believe you can just throw up any old picture and a few paragraphs about your cat...there is a method to online dating and talking about your cat ain't one of em!

Texting!!!! - I could write a book about this, but wait... I already have! This medium is absolutely huge and most of you have no idea how to use it correctly. If you are the least bit curious about texting and how to DOMINATE, take a look. http://www.amazon.com/TextAppeal-Ultimate-Texting-Guide-ebook/dp/B0034XS728

Email - Email is a bit of a pathetic form of communication for dating. I don't recommend it since it takes so long to go back and forth. Using email to get to know someone is a great way for both partners to get frustrated and eventually lose attraction. If someone wants to chat via email I will usually get them to text me, or IM me (instant messaging.) Keep the email to a minimum and move into something a bit quicker.

Skype/Video chat - I have to admit I really like Skype! When I lived in Japan I bought a Skype number in the US that my family could call, this local number would forward to my Japanese number and family/friends could call anytime they wanted. When I was separated from my girlfriend for three months we talked via Video Skype almost nightly (and had a little online sex to boot). Skype is a great way to IM and is wonderful for the long distance relationship. (Am I the only one wondering about Skype sex? And how I can get some?!)

IM - Instant messaging is often one of the initial steps in getting to know someone. It is excellent practice for those of you that feel a bit nervous about face-to-face conversation, or you don't really know enough and you want to be a bit cautious. I like to use skype for my IM interactions or the Facebook chat client. IM-ing can be a great way to chat, the only problem is that he might not be responding to your every message and you are left waiting for his response and that sucks.

Facebook - Just like everyone else I have embraced Facebook and if you haven't yet what is wrong with you?! Facebook is an EXCELLENT vehicle for dating. Let's say you meet a guy and you want to connect with him some more you don't have to say the embarrassing, "What's your number?" All you have to do is invite him to your Facebook page and drop him an email. For some strange reason people like to collect Facebook friends like baseball cards and I don't think I have ever had anyone say no. Facebook is a very non-intimidating way to get to know someone without any pretense. Why else is it so great for dating?
- If he turns out to be a creeper you can easily block him from Facebook
- You can post tons of flattering Photos of yourself for him to fantasize over
- You can learn a bit more about him without him knowing…
- Neither of you have to accept a friend request and it is a nice way to avoid giving your number

- You are pretty insulated on Facebook and if you spend the time to understand it you can control exactly what he sees
- It is so much easier than asking for a phone number, which the girl shouldn't do anyway
- It shows interest but not necessarily sexual, it won't send the wrong message
- You can easily drop him a message on his wall or a comment on his status to gauge his interest, he doesn't respond? Well now you know.

Twitter - I have been using Twitter for over a year now and I still don't know what the heck it is or how to use it. I have met a few people here but I don't think it is a good dating/talking medium. Let me know if you find otherwise.

Dating, Sex, and Relationship Blogs - Online resources-especially dating blogs-now more than ever provide an absolute TON of information for any dating conundrum that you may be facing.

There are e-books, instant downloadable MP3s, videos, dating coaches, relationship coaches, matchmakers, Doctors and therapist all online waiting to help you find love!

Both Kim and I run blogs on dating that are wonderful resources for dating. I suggest you take advantage of them.   http://www.mikethemasterdater.com   and http://www.kimhess.com But I'm sure you are already a fan, right? RIGHT?!

Mike is right communication has really changed as in: Text, Facebook, online dating sites, email, IM, smoke signals, morse code.... But really, there are so many ways to communicate while dating it gets to be a bit much. I've had a potential date

142

say he actually lost track of our communication because we would "speak" to each other using three different communication methods without ever hearing the others' voice. He eventually ended up calling me (on an actual phone!) to set a date…or a non-date, not sure which it was even though he walked me home and I did wear heels!

It used to be two people went to dinner at a nice restaurant and then to a movie. Over dinner these two people got to know one another. "How many brothers and sisters do you have?" and "What do you do for a living," and so on. Now all that's pretty much gone because much of the communicating is done before the date. This is usually done to see if the other person is worth the time in your busy schedule. If they are deemed acceptable, you know so much about them already that the conversation you would have had over dinner has already been discussed or found out through Google, and creepin' on his Facebook page.

No Standard

And let's talk about the old standard dinner and a movie, not so standard anymore. The formality of a dinner date has been replaced with grabbing a drink, either coffee or alcohol. This is done to assess whether the potential date is worth more than an hour of the askee's time. I've gotta admit, I kinda like suggesting drinks for a possible first meeting. I believe this is done by both men and women to suggest a certain nonchalantness. (Or, the guy is just cheap. I'm betting on cheap!)

Are you dating anyone?

If someone asks "Are you dating someone" used to be an easy question to answer. Yes or no. It's like asking if you're pregnant! Well, it used to be. Now with the changes in dating it can be difficult to define a relationship. There are "friends with benefits" which means they are friends, and you have sex with them but may not date. Or you hang out with them (dinner and a movie anyone?) then have sex, but you don't call the other person your boyfriend or girlfriend. What about online dating? I've known people who chat and correspond with one person and one person only for months through online dating sites. They may even go out with them 3 or 4 times. Are they dating? Or what about the person who is having several relationships that are ongoing instead of one intimate commitment. "Are you dating someone?" is not as simple a question as it once was!

The purpose of dating used to be all about a very basic idea. Getting to know someone and find compatibility for a long-term commitment. Now people not only date to find a relationship, but to find out more about themselves! What they want, what they don't want, what they need or deserve in relation to how the date treated them…kind of like getting therapy and a possible relationship all in one!

The Mini date and the Non-Date

This is one of largest changes in dating that you probably have no idea about and something we will expand on further in a later section. Certain things that once were considered dating are now categorized as just meeting up, hanging out, or my fave the mini date or the "the non-date." In case you're wondering,

The Urban Dictionary defines non-date as:
It is basically dating without the entitlement. There is no pressure, yet at the same time, both non-daters refuse to flirt with others. Often a precursor to dating.

The Non-date is a little bit different than what a mini date is but they two tend to intertwine, we are more interested in teaching you about the Mini date but I want you to be aware of the Non-date as well.

Non-date? WTF?

Here, my friends, is one utterly crazy thing that has changed in the dating world! Before I got married, there was no such thing as a "mini-date" or "non-date." Now, 13 years back into the dating game, I find out that I can have a guy ask me out for coffee, I can accept, get dolled up, put makeup on, we have said coffee, he asks when we can hang out again, and then I learn that this was not a date. Then what is? What are the rules? Does it have to be after 7:00pm? Must there be some form of eating involved? Does he have to pick me up? Is it a "mini-Date/non-date" if I wear flats instead of heels? Is that a date or a non-date?

Whatever you wanna call it, treat it as a casual/fun meeting to see if he could possibly be the father of your 10 children. Keep it light and see if you like the guy before making a big deal out of it.

Video: The Mini Date
http://www.startdatingagain.net/?page_id=66
Learn a little bit more about how dating has changed because of the Internet.

XII. Dating details - The mini date and exit strategies

First date: where/what/how!?

You met someone you like, what do you do? Invite him over for a romantic dinner? Go to Taco Bell to show you are not too serious? No, to either, Let me show you how it is done.

Real date or Mini date?

This is very simple if you can say NO to any of these go on a Mini date first:

- Have you met in person?
- Spent more than 4 hours on the phone?
- Know FOR SURE he is single?
- Seen a full body shot and MULTIPLE pictures of him? (Facebook is great for this)

If you can say YES to any of these, go on a Mini date first:

- Are you feeling a bit needy and sexually lonely?
- Seen less than ten photos of him?
- Had sexual conversations already?
- Falsely imagine that he is a keeper?
- He is a little bit shady about ANYTHING?

Whatever you decide make sure you error on the side of caution. Remember the last thing you want to do is

146

let some creepy dude have your phone number or worse yet, know where you live. Take your time, if he is into you he will have the respect to wait.

From meeting to Mini Dates to the Real Date

The typical progression from meeting to mini date to real date:

1. Contact (Online personals, Twitter, Mutual friends)
2. Email/IM – IM is probably safer and more flexible
3. Texting – can be a whole lot of fun and I think and excellent arena for banter
4. Phone call – a couple times at least
5. Skype/video call can be excluded but is an EXCELLENT way to find out if he really looks like what he says
6. Coffee/Lunch – This is the key step that most people omit. Meet him for coffee during the day and see if the two of you fit. Make sure to tell him you have to meet someone shortly after, just in case he only has one arm and is 20 years older than his picture.
7. Drinks? - This could sub for coffee but it is much harder to escape. Not only that but most men associate drinks with sex, something you don't want in his head just yet. If you have to go this route make sure you have a time limit. I made this mistake recently and I was stuck with a girl that tried to get a second date out of me by inviting me do go drunken deer hunting with her, Seriously! (I should have done it)
8. Mini date – A dinner at a local hole in the wall or something fun like ice-skating. This is the time to let go a little bit and see if he is the kind of guy you

want to take to the next level. I would have a couple of these before you progress to the next level.

9. Real Date! – Pretty similar to above but with one key difference. You have accepted him and are ready to become physical. This is why you don't talk about sex early on! We are building up to this point and if it comes up too soon you will sleep with him too soon and that is bad bad bad!! After the date, I think it is much better to end up at his house rather than yours. This shows that he doesn't have a live-in girlfriend or wife! (You would be surprised) This also shows that he takes you a seriously enough to bring you into his home, which shows his interest clearly.

10. Repeat and be cautious!! – If you have followed the steps correctly and actually gotten here, I imagine the guy is actually a keeper. If you are cautious, it will filter out the guys that are willing to say anything and everything in order to get your panties off. Take your time and show you are serious about what you want.

What if we've met before?

If you have met him before and know him a little bit this radically changes things. Let's assume that he is physically, mentally, and financially acceptable. You have basically covered steps 1-6 so now we can jump to step seven or the mini date if you desire.

1. Drinks/(coffee/lunch) – Get to know him a bit more and see what makes him tick. Try to ask a lot of questions, it will put you in control of the conversation, give him something to talk about and stop you from making an ass of yourself if you are nervous. Make sure that this mini date has a time/drink limit of two (two drinks or two hours). You

guys are hitting it off!? NO?? Smack yourself on the muzzle and leave.
2. Mini date – Same as above
3. Real date – same as above
4. Repeat

Exit Strategy

Remember to always, always have an exit strategy!

- 2 hours and/or 2 drinks

Set the expectation before the mini-date that you will be leaving in two hours or just have time for a couple of drinks. This shows you have a life and he should feel privileged to have gotten some of your time!

- 1 hour is lame - A one-hour date doesn't give you much time to learn about or interact with your date. If someone said they only had an hour for you would you even bother meeting up?

- 3 hours/3 drinks shows too much interest on your part. Remember men instinctively like to chase. Also, anything more than 3 drinks puts you into the danger zone where your judgment will get impaired and you are appearing as if you are looking for sex. If you don't set clear boundaries you will end up not in control and without the guy.

Who asks out who?

As a general rule the guy should always be the one to ask the girl out. Guys are the chasers and girls are the choosers. You may be thinking that this is a new era and women should be allowed to ask guys out!!! NO!

149

NO NO NO NO!! Please watch the video below to understand why both Kim and I feel very strongly about this.

Video: Asking him out?
http://www.startdatingagain.net/?page_id=62
This is something that most relationship experts are just flat WRONG about. Find out the best way to get him to go out with you.

Rules of who should pay

So you are at the restaurant or bar and the rules for who pays are not yet established. What do you do?? Go dutch? Or rotate? Or just let him pay every time? Since a lot of people are very opinionated on this topic I am going to tell you what is most appropriate from THE GUYS point of view.

Dutch

Going dutch is for friends, not for dates. If he suggests this I would be a tad wary. He is either ultra poor or hasn't dated very often.

Let him pay most of the time?

Most guys will and should offer to pay for the first date...but every date? I am still shocked and mildly disgusted that some women still think this is appropriate! This type of thinking is incredibly hypocritical. Sorry ladies, gone is the time of the 1950's male that opened doors for you but also gone is the white picket fenced house wife and unequal pay.

Who should pay for a date? I believe the man should pay for the first date. He asked, he should pay. Does that mean I believe he should pay for every date? Nah. On the first date I feel it's appropriate for a man to pay for dinner. I will offer to pay for the tip or pick up the drinks or dessert if we go somewhere afterwards.

Now if he gets the bill and asks me "So how should we do this" or says "Your half is…" I will be truly disgusted. You should too. C'mon it's dinner, not a trip to Paris! If he can't be kind and considerate enough to treat you to one lousy dinner…he's not worthy of your precious time.

Whoever asks the other out pays

This is acceptable but you really shouldn't be the one asking him out, so in other word he should be the one paying for the first date. Does that mean he pays for the whole night, of drinks bowling, dinner… Maybe, but I would certainly offer to start rotating right away. What does this mean? If he buys a round at a bar, you buy the round at the next bar.

Why rotating?

So let's assume that he has asked you out and he steps up to pay for the first date. As the woman you should expect to pay for the next date. Even if they guy insists, I want you to do this for a few reasons:

- If you always let him pay you and he, will feel that something is owed and that usually involves sex.
- Even if he insists he often doesn't mean it and is just trying to appear to be the guy his mother raised. However, he will eventually feel resentment at having to cough up $ at every date.

- Even if he really truly does want to pay every time, is this what you want? Do you want to set that precedent for the rest of the relationship? You, owing him?

I highly respect the woman that will go back and forth with me but do I keep score? Sometimes! After being put into mild credit card debt in my early 20's by a girl demanding I pay for everything I won't go there again! The reason why I think this is so important is because it sets a very fair expectation for the rest of the relationship. He wants to know that he has a partner not a subordinate. This is also something that you must want for yourself, not to be treated as a subordinate! Sharing the cost of your dates seems like a trivial thing but I believe it is very important to establish a healthy balance right away. So let's reiterate.

- Let him pay for the first date (if he hints at dutch say, "You get this and I will get the next time.")
- Rotate who pays (It's that simple)

Video: Who Pays??
http://www.startdatingagain.net/?page_id=57
Kim and I butt head again over who should pay for the date but I think we agree in the long run.

eDating – Going on that first date
By Kim Hess

You've been scouring the online ads for days, weeks, months and now and you are exhausted. You are ready to throw in the hat, and give up online dating-for real this time!

You feel you have great qualities and are just looking for a man who is your equal and will respect your quirky sense of humor. What are you finding instead? Men who write and spell worse than a 3rd grader, who claim that their friends put them up to this, or complain that women are evil gold diggers who only want to make their life miserable like their ex who broke up with him 2 months ago.

Most of the men have the typical crappy profile: the opening line of–"I don't know what to put here, so just ask me," cheesy photos from 3 years ago and the generic declarations of love for the beach, coffee, and the T.V. show "24". And just as you're about to quit internet dating–once and for all–you see mail in your inbox. You decide, what the heck, can't be any worse than the ultra-conservative, tax hating, gun toting guy in the wheelchair who was surrounded by four busty American flag bikini clad blondes in his profile picture (ladies, this happened to me!) You check it only to find a short and funny message from a man who's DOESN'T WRITE IN ALL CAPS, uses none of the tired clichés, and appears as if he actually read your entire profile, instead of just scanning your age and pictures.

You reply, email back and forth, start texting or using IM (instant messaging) and he calls to ask you out. Boom: you got yourself a date. Here are some guidelines to follow before you both actually meet:

No fantasizing!
Don't start imagining the witty conversation you will share, the romantic kiss at the end of the night or what your party favors for your wedding reception will be. Stop this train of thought right now! Don't build the guy up and you won't be disappointed if he turns out to have less personality than Donald Trump.

Don't Obsess!
Do not keep talking about your date to friends, on Facebook or Twitter. Don't text him everyday telling him you can't wait to meet him, giving him turn-by-turn directions to the restaurant, or telling him you had toast

for breakfast. Do what you normally do and put him and your date on the backburner. I know you're excited but you had a life before this date and you'll have a life after this date!

Don't go too fast!
No need to tell your date when you chat on the phone that you prefer missionary to doggy style. Don't ask him about his ex, or tell him about yours. Please, for the love of God, don't ask him where he's thinking about going for the second date or if he's free for the 4th of July when you haven't yet met him!

Let's NOT get dirty!
No sexy photos (you know those full frontal shots I'm talkin' about!) suggestive hints or phone sex. This will give him a pass to attempt to get into your pants on the first date. Just say no!

Mystery...have some
No need to know how much is in his 401K plan and what his kindergarten teacher's name was. No need to tell him about your cat's veterinarian appointment or your bra size. Men love mystery and telling too much too soon can leave the first date interaction boring.

Following all of these tips (I said ALL, not some!) will leave you sparkling, interesting, and ready for your first date!

How to make your first date really kick butt!

It is very possible your first date with him might be awful but that is a good thing! You and your personality is a sieve for the kind of guy you want. The most honest and real you are with him the sooner you can find out if you have a prince or a frog. I think the most common mistake any guy or girl does on the first date is to force attraction. This is often a waste of time, if the chemistry isn't there initially it most certainly never will be. Accept that he might be unacceptable and move on quickly. However, with that said we want to create the best atmosphere possible for you to figure this out.

1. Be yourself, he doesn't like it? You are down one more frog – Do I need to go into this again? You got it right? It is a good thing to filter one more guy out.
2. Don't be afraid to call him out on his bullshit – Calling people on their garbage is hugely attractive. Don't hesitate to disagree with him, of course do so in a conversational way and obviously, ex-talk, politics and religion are things to steer him away from! Don't let him screw up the date either.
3. Ask questions, don't talk so much! – Let him entertain you, since this is really the role he should be playing anyway. Recently, while doing some online dating I was blown away with how many Chatty Cathys I talked to. I am not sure if they were nervous, but all I could do was listen to them talk and talk and talk... I never called them back. You are the chooser he is the chaser, encourage him to be the one to put his foot in his mouth or possibly impress you?
4. Be witty, be opinionated – I don't know where this came from, but the 1980's idiot busty blond inundated with men is ridiculous! Show him that you have a brain, have the guts to have an opinion! This is why bitches and dicks are so successful at dating, they have power and power is sexy. Throw down a strong opinion and see if he can hurdle it without falling apart, great filtering technique and attraction builder
5. Let him make the advances that you can turn down – A girl making advances on a guy is odd to say the least. He might be a little hunk cake that you want to savor every slice of but STOP!! Once again you are the chased, he is the one impressing you. Allow and encourage him to make advances and then either accept or hint at a rain check.

155

6. Keeping the sex talk to a minimum – But still be sexy. We want to elicit from a man proper behavior first, so please don't fall into the trap of sex-talk too soon! Most guys will initiate a little sex talk immediately to gauge the possibility. Make sure to not respond if it is showing up already. Allowing sex talk right away will unfailingly send him down the wrong path of expectation and you switch from "potential mate" to only "mate". Please don't hesitate to be sexy this is the bait on your hook but it is essential that you don't let him nibble yet.

7. NO Negative Talk! – I will actually stop a date and scold a girl for negative self-talk. I explain how it makes me feel towards her, how much it ruins my image of her. Negative self-talk is the bacterial rot that not only destroys your life but also kills attraction faster than a live toad in a microwave. (I am ashamed to say I actually did this at age 12, it was a mess)

8. Start slowly – Do mini dates, and don't be in a hurry! To help this out make sure you are having mini dates with many people. You don't need to be sleeping with any of them but by having them in your life it insulates you from paying too much attention to any one guy. Don't scare the fish away by yanking on the pole so soon. Ignore your hunger and be patient. Start slow, date many, and only accept the best.

9. Have zero expectations – Have you ever heard the expression, "A watched pot never boils"? Why? When you place too much expectation on something, you send out a repulsive vibe. The repulsive vibe is one of loss and need, the last thing you want to put out towards an attractive guy.

10. Dress appropriate! – I met a girl once while racing a 10K, we chatted a bit after the race and decided to

meet again. A week later we met for lunch she was dressed as if we were going clubbing in Vegas. This was bloody lunch and I was wearing shorts and a tee shirt! Clearly, we had very different views as to what this meant to us. Her over dressing for a café looked needy and a bit pathetic. Look good, but by looking too good you could kill it. (Kim tells me for a lunch date, cute jeans and an adorable top works. For evening, maybe something a little more feminine like a modest dress and heels. Remember this is a first date, not an audition for "The Bachelor!")

11. Don't like him? Don't waste your time! – Life is limited, don't be afraid to just move the hell on. Saying "no" is a muscle most of us need to flex more often. He probably knows as well that the two of you are not very well suited is just hanging on for the possibility of sex.

XII. Let's talk about sex - About time!

Wo hoo! We finally get to my favorite section! SEX! I adore sex and I certainly hope you do too because it is a pretty damn important next step

...and lots of fun!

You own your sex life

I want to jump in here before Mike takes you on his wild and fun journey of sex! I cannot stress enough the importance of owning your sexuality. Most women, from birth, are given the ideas and so-called morals that "good" girls don't enjoy sex or even have sex!

I subscribed to this theory having grown up in a religious household. The only thing my parents said to me about sex was, "If you ever start taking birth control, I don't want to know about it." I don't want to cast my parental figures in a harsh light...they loved me. I imagine they loved me so much they didn't want to imagine their daughter having to experience any of the fear, hurt feelings, or consequences of sexual activity. Of course they were only focusing on the bad: teenage pregnancy, sexually transmitted diseases and infections, emotional pain from hurt feelings and so on.

They failed to communicate to me the joys of having a wonderful proud sexuality and the good that sex brings to one's life. The physical pleasure, the release, the high, the connection, the spirituality, the passion. I'm writing all this because I want to communicate this to you in a strong way.

I want to eradicate the notion of having sex to please a man and a man only. You should have sex because it feels good. Because you want to. Because you want to express your love (or lust). If you have any guilt about sex, let's start to work on getting that negative emotion out of your life now. Your sexuality is a gift for you to enjoy, to relish, using as much or little as you like. There is no one that has dominion over your sex life now...work it!

Caution...

So far I have told you to error on the side of caution when it comes to sex. Guys are on the hunt for it, no matter what age, or culture. If the hunt was too easy they rarely hang around after. We need not only to become challenging prey but to also stay on our guard to maintain mutual interest.

I would like to make this a bit of an FAQ since I have already laid out a lot of my rules for sleeping with a guy. Here are many of the questions I get most often.

Q: How soon do I have sex after meeting?

A: I would say no sooner than the 3rd or 4th date. This amount of time usually weeds out the guys that only have sex on the brain. Once these guys are gone it is usually fine to take things to the next level. Although this is something you really need to sense for yourself. A lot of women tell me they make guys wait a month or longer! But do **you** really want to wait that long? Do you think he will wait that long?

I agree with Mike about waiting for the 3rd or 4th date. If you want to wait a month or longer go for it. Be realistic and know he may not stick around for that long, but you have your reasons right? If your reason is to use sex as a manipulative weapon, stop right now. Go with your intuition and your feelings for the guy. Sex is to be enjoyed not doled out as reward or withheld as punishment.

Q: He told me he has a three date minimum for sex, how should I respond?

A: Well this guy figured out the advice above! For him to communicate this to you is like saying, "Hey can you skip the whole talking part so that we can have sex now?" Obviously this guy is a big NO, his only interest is in sex and he probably combs the online dating circuit to get his groove on.

A: Tell him that's nice and don't return his phone calls, no matter how cute. He doesn't respect you and sees you as something to masturbate in and nothing else. Don't be his replacement for a blow up doll.

Q: We had sex recently and I felt as if my feelings were not reciprocated, should I continue?

A: This is one of the bummers about sex, men and women are wired so differently. Men just don't have the same hormonal releases after sex UNLESS they are really into you. Women almost always have a strong surge of oxytocin (the love hormone) following sex. For men it is hard to tell what happens after sex (oxytocin is hard to measure because the male orgasm is much shorter) but I can conjecture that it really depends on how he was feeling before the sex.

160

I believe that if he deep down considers you an acceptable and desirable long term mate he allows that hormone to over take his system. A man that doesn't? I think it is instantly doused after sex, and he wakes up and heads for the door. This is why we want to take our time to make sure attraction is real because the man may not be able to differentiate between liking you or wanting to sleep with you. But, if you're honest with yourself, you can probably tell, even if he can't

Q: After we had sex he just disappeared, what happened?

A: Very closely related to the answer above but I need a little more to go on. There are many reasons why you get a "hit and run" the major ones are:

- You slept with him too soon
- He was too attractive for you (He didn't consider you his equal)
- This is kinda what he does, and you were a sexual target
- He has a wife/girlfriend
- He didn't have deeper feelings and the sex satisfied his only desire
- You didn't have any positive sexual tension and attraction died
- Negative tension fueled the interaction (pretty much the same as above)
- You were bad in bed? (doubtful, unless he is highly experienced)

Guys disappear for only one reason, they are too afraid to face you. That fear is usually based out of some sort of guilt or confusion. You see, most men don't know how they feel in the moment. They may think that they are into you, but the second they have sex they realize that they were only into sex. Guys are often as clueless about this as you are; this is why it is sickening to many men when their attraction shuts off like a blackout. This is another reason to take things slow, if his sexual attraction for you is trumping his mental attraction there is no way to maintain the relationship and he will inevitably disappear.

A: I had to add something here: guys are too afraid to face you because most women they've dealt with have been over emotional and crazy! I've been that girl, you've been that girl, and the guy that disappears has dealt with that girl. No one wants to deal with someone who's crazy. Even if you're not crazy now, he doesn't know that. Leave him alone. In my experience with men that disappear, most likely he'll be back and by then you'll have moved on to the next one. That is such a good point Kim!

Q: We were intimately involved a few times but he keeps getting texts while we're are together, is he involved with another woman?

A: This is something that so many women don't get. Women make the assumption that sex equals exclusivity. Men on the other hand assume that sex is sex and the more the merrier. Since neither party wants to have the sexual exclusivity talk, each makes opposite assumptions about the meaning of sex. I can promise you, without a shadow of a doubt, if it is not CLEAR he will sleep with any and all takers until it is made clear.

Is there another woman? Probably! What do I do? Be honest with him and yourself. Maybe you don't want exclusivity now either but are just being tricked by your genitals?

A: Sweetheart, hell yeah he's involved with someone else! You think that's his Grandma texting him while you're together? No, you're a grown ass woman, who knows what's what. You're not exclusive unless you both agree to be exclusive. In the meantime, get out and start dating other men and if so inclined get "involved" with another man. It will take the desperate and needy smell off of you.

Q: Should I disclose to a man that I am sleeping with more men than just him?

A: No. He wouldn't with you, why should you to him? If he wants more let him make that clear to you. Otherwise, love it up!

A: Ditto. Doubl ditto!

Q: I disagree with you that I need to wait so long before I sleep with a man; I get fine results with the first date!

A: I agree that you disagree! And you are right. I only lay down the ground rules because they are the easiest for most people to follow. It is very possible to sleep with him the first night and retain him but you got to have some serious game. Since most of you don't have that kind of game or even want it, I would suggest going with what makes you feel the most comfortable.

A: I've had sex with a few guys on the first date that lasted many months, and a few that have lasted many years as friends. I've also slept with a few guys on the first date that I never saw again. Let's just say the odds ain't 50/50. My opinion...it's not worth the risk of having sex on the first date if you want a second date.

Q: I haven't had sex with another man besides my husband in 10 years, I am nervous!

A: Good, how exciting! Make sure you realize that you will be on an emotional rollercoaster ride for the first few men until you can get back in the game. In other words, be on guard against the emotions that will come flooding out of the excitement of a new relationship.

A: What Mike is trying to tell you is that because you're a woman you're gonna fall in love with the first few men you sleep with. I did it, but I had no one to warn me. I'm warning you. Enjoy it and keep in the back of your mind that this man does NOT have to become your next boyfriend for life.

As far as being nervous, you'll be fine. You're allowing this man to pleasure you and this should be a fun and enjoyable time. Use your nerves to excite yourself with the newness of a new man in your bed. Gotta tell you it is great after 10, 20 30 years of the same man day after day, year after year!

Q: I am tired of meeting men that are bad lovers, is there any way to speed up this process? Any questions I can ask??

A: This is one of my favorite questions!! Unfortunately it is a question that is very very hard to answer! I think someone should setup a secret website just for women called rateaguy.com this way you can just look up what his previous sexual stats were. But... it doesn't exist yet and probably a good thing because I get enough dates already!

164

So how do you know... how do you know...?? That is really a tough one! And I answer questions like I play pool, I always try to make a shot!!
I think there might be a few indicators:

- He is creative
- Has the desire to please
- Clear clean confidence
- Radiates sexuality in a non sleazy way
- Doesn't need to talk about sex (I would be an exception)
- Is able to take physical liberties with you, WITHOUT making you uncomfortable (Sexual and non-sexual)
- You just have a feeling!
- You feel ridiculously comfortable with him
- He had to pry his ex-girlfriend off with pepper stray and a tazer

Obviously there really is no way to tell since a lot of guys are like limping pigeons... One pigeon gets fed because it is limping, so the entire flock learns the behavior. Hard to assume his act is authentic when sex is on the line.

Q: I haven't used birth control for 10 years!! Is this something he will take care of? What do I use? Do I have to worry about STIs/STDs?

A: Oh gosh... I really don't want to answer this because sometimes I am not the most responsible person. I think you already know the answer to this, put a condom on the guy (really no substitute) and make sure his peter looks healthy, since a condom won't stop HPV or herpes. I could go on and on and on and on but

165

would it really matter? There is no reason to create panic over something you will forget when he is going down on you and has forgotten protection.

Be responsible as much as you are comfortable with, until you get a nice raging case of Gonorrhea or Chlamydia. That will teach you better than anything I say here. Fortunately for those of us over the age of thirty STI's start to decline radically.

A: You DON'T have to get gonorrhea to learn how to be responsible! Always, always have your partner wear a condom because you don't know where his penis has been! Take care of yourself too. Make an appointment with your doctor or nurse after you've researched a few options. You're a grown woman, this is sooo simple.

And if he tells you he doesn't wear condoms, let him know you don't have sex without them! Your health and life is worth one billion times more than a one time sexual encounter.

I guess this is the pessimist in me, I am such a negative Nancy since so few people listen. Yeah, this is a pretty serious deal, one that could cost you your life or have you forever on herpessingles.com. Don't be this girl. (Just to give you a bit of a scare, my closest friend just contracted herpes, the scary thing is he probably got it months ago, multiple partners back. Now he has to disclose to any woman he sleeps with and the condom ain't 100% with herpes. He is now in sexual purgatory, a place none of us wants to be.)

Q: I just had a rough night with him not being able to get it up, is it me? What can I do to arouse him more?

A: There are many reasons for a guy's stuff to not work. If he is over the age of 40 it is most likely lack of fitness or age. If he is under that I would assume that he contracted a nice case of performance anxiety. What can you do? Have a little Viagra in your purse? Why the hell not? You have condoms and lube in there, right!?

The take away message would be, don't take it personally, and don't be cruel. If it happens again, just move on kindly.

A: It's not you, it's him.

Video: Exploring your sexuality
http://www.startdatingagain.net/?page_id=73
Back in the sexual game, what is new? What to expect? How to have really really great sex!

How coming out of a long relationship has given you advantages

I want you to understand something; you are not coming into the dating world totally unprepared. You are entering the dating world again with a lot more knowledge, self-assurance and maturity. You know the mistakes you don't wish to repeat, and you understand men a thousand times better! You probably are far more comfortable with your sexuality, although a little more of it might have been nice. You have grown and have a lot of experience over men that have never been in a long-term relationship. Simply put, although you have suffered you have gained so much more. I hope that you can reframe this experience into something that is preparing you for and ever-greater journey.

20 Killer tips to be AMAZING in bed
By Mike Masters

1. *Adore sex – if a girl is not a fan of sex it pretty much kills the whole thing. The guy might get to a happy place but he might as well be masturbating. Adoring sex with him is not only incredible for you but will create a superglue like bond between the two of you and make you both* better in bed.

2. *Be wild and spontaneous (have sex anywhere and everywhere) – Every girl that I remember being amazing in bed wanted to get down anywhere and everywhere. At times this was obnoxious and I had to explain to one girl that a packed movie theater was not the place for a hand job.*

3. *Have a powerful orgasm – One of the biggest turn-ons for most men is to see a woman having an orgasm. I am not talking about a little hiccup of one that skips along every 5 minutes but a force five GALE of an orgasm that shakes the foundations of the house. If you are not having these, you need to seek out some help!*

4. *Always be willing to make love – I have a rule, NEVER SAY NO. Of course if one person has a fever of 104 I might only do a quickie but in general I severely enforce this. Having this rule not only makes sex better but it stops negative feelings from forming if one partner refuses the other.*

5. *Become excellent at telling him what to do – You just gotta do this… not explaining what you like does both of you a huge disservice. Don't be shy, if you like vegetables in bed then let him know! Also don't forget to constantly probe him (not literally) for what he likes, often even guys are a little shy about sex.*

6. *Wanting to please him as much as possible – This falls under the law of reciprocity. Please him and he will want to please you, of course if you feel it is getting too one sided let the selfish bastard know! I personally can't stand a girl that does not reciprocate in bed.*

7. *Screw him back – If you are too passive in bed he might as well buy a blow up doll. It may not seem like it but you could be doing a whole lot more in missionary. I have been amazed by what a little movement in the right way can do for sex. I once was with a girl that could take me over the edge nearly instantly while on top, something that no other girl was able to do. (She was in my top five)*

8. *Proper dirty talk – If you are not having at least a little dirty pillow talk you are missing out! It is just plain sexy when girls* talk dirty in bed, *even sexier if there is a thick accent involved!*

168

9. *Taking on a passive role* – Sometimes it is pretty attractive to let him just take you. To let him use you aggressively, just to get off. Let him be selfish every once in a while and let him know you like it.

10. *Taking on an aggressive role* – I love it when a girl takes the male role and has her way with me. A girl I dated got off of work at two in the morning and would come over to my house and jump me while I was half asleep. It was wonderful...

11. *Showing zero aversion to spermies* – You think his stuff is disgusting? Well, not only will the make him shy about his natural functions but it will kill more adventurous sex and many of his fantasies. Sure it tastes like ass and smells like bleach but so what, get over it. Do you think you are always roses down there? Get as comfortable as you possibly can with his junk and you will be surprised at the results.

12. *Share pornography time* – You may not be into porn but I can almost promise you that he is. If you can share this part of his life periodically, without jealousy, it will bring you closer. I am not asking you to watch some nasty stuff that you are morally opposed to but to find something that both of you can enjoy. It wouldn't hurt to have him "catch" you watching something dirty sometime.

13. *Using toys together* – This very well might be one of his fantasies, why have you been hiding that vibrator out of embarrassment? Guys like toys and are fascinated with your privates. If you let him dig around in your sandbox a bit I can almost promise you it will turn him on like mad.

14. *Understanding his comfort zone* – A lot of the things I have suggested are great around someone like me that has seen and done most things. However, if you are with an inexperienced guy you may not want to pull out the Ben-wa balls quite yet. I met a girl once that wanted to pee on me, needless to say I didn't see her again (well after we had sex).

15. *Get "caught" doing something bad* – This is a great thing to do if you want to shock his sexual system. I walked in to my room after work once to find my girlfriend on her stomach, butt naked, and masturbating as blatantly as my mom's cockatiel. I about died and couldn't get my clothes off fast enough. God, she was *good fun in bed!*

16. *Tease him when it is inappropriate* – Teasing him when there is nothing he can do about is excellent foreplay, a place like church or parents house just adds to the spice. Make sure you keep it up every five minutes until you get him to a place where he can do something about it (I once got a hand job in a packed Chemistry lab, at a Christian college by the Dean's daughter, Wow...)

169

17. *Dress sexy and take care of yourself* – this is something I learned from Japanese woman. They always looked their best and I have to admit Western girls could learn a lot from this. Girls walking around in their sweats with greasy hair and frumpy clothes are not very sexy. Sure, when you are at home let your hair down but don't get too comfortable if he is there. One of the things that kills attraction is when couples let themselves slide and then the sex follows. This rule applies to guys too and you have my permission to tell them.

18. *Remove the distractions* – This is closely related to looking sexy but it is a little more graphic, even a few of my best lovers have instantly ruined attraction with nasty distractions. The biggest one is smell; if a girl has a bad smell down south or bad breath it kills everything. Sure he might still have sex with you but the black cloud of your stench will be looming in the back of his mind and he will be a bit disgusted. Don't forget... hair on the nipples, ungroomed genitals, left over toilet paper

19. *Stay in shape!* – I am guilty of this just like most of us. We get into a relationship and we let ourselves go because we are comfortable with the other person. Unfortunately if the girl he originally met suddenly has a different body I can promise you it will impact his attraction to you. No offense, but if he starts looking like a biggest loser contestant you won't feel like having sex with him either.

20. *Train him to be* better in bed *– I once was with a girl that loved to bring me over a few times before she was done with me. This conditioned me to want to have 2-3 orgasms with her every time we were intimate. This not only was better for me but for both of us. She got more lovin and I enjoyed not just popping once and falling asleep. She demanded better sex and got it (Just found out she is getting engaged, would it be inappropriate to attend her bachelorette party?)*

Preparation Bullets:

Wow, we really killed it on this chapter! An absolute ton of info and some disagreement from Kim and I over casual sex, but I think you find a pretty united front on all other topics.

This is the chapter of execution, and it should be painfully clear what to expect and how to take the first steps but lets reintroduce the major points just to be sure.

- Recreational dating is something that I push but Kim resists. I feel this is a very personal choice and it really comes down to your own wiring. If you are cool with it go have fun, if not, be patient. Just be aware that most men ONLY want to recreationally date.
- Getting yourself back out there will involve a little pain, you won't find "him" immediately and having sex again might be emotionally challenging. This is to be expected and is part of the process. I personally find the process so much fun, be patient and promise me NOT to give up from only a couple of bad dates.
- Finding a great guy means not putting expectation or attention on him. This is why it is so helpful to be "fishing" for many men at the same time. It insulates you emotionally, increases your chances, keeps your attention split, and makes ALL the guys far more interested.
- Online dating may be your only option, if so I hope you enter with your head on strait. Many men consider online dating like shooting fish in a barrel, if you don't want to be one of those fish, error on the side of caution and use the mini date as a way to filter the scumbags.
- I hope you can meet people offline because this really is where the great people are. I think the most important message of this chapter is that you shouldn't be actively looking but you should be actively BEING. Take your separation as a rebirth, a phoenix from the flames, this is your life, not your exes. It is time to reset, restart and be reborn. The better you feel about yourself the greater quality man you will draw.
- Do I really need to tell you to bring your own condoms? Remember my buddy that just contracted herpes? Just do it, and here is a little tidbit: If you have the balls to stop him and demand he use a condom, you just set a boundary, you showed power and increased attraction.

- You don't have time... Please... How many worthless things do you do everyday. Turn off that damn TV, throw away the romance novels, stop checking facebook every ten minutes and get the hell out of the house. Hell, take a three month vacation to Thailand, it will only run you about 4,000 US, make a bloody change for once! You want a better life? A better man? Make some damn changes!!! Now go tell your excuses to go F themselves.
- I know you probably know all about using FB or texting or skype, or do you? This might be how you do the majority of your communication. Don't underestimate how powerful your behavior is perceived digitally, and it is more often than not misunderstood.
- Error on the side of caution, not only is it simply wise, but a cautious woman is interesting to all men. It puts them on their best behavior, attraction is increased, and it simply is safer. Use the mini date as often as you can, stalk their facebook. Hell, you might even want to be like my psycho friend and google them. (Amazingly she finds dirt on almost all the guys)
- Always have an exit strategy. A friend calling, emergency, an appointment, ANYTHING. Coming to the first date without one is like, forgetting your condoms. Don't do it, just not safe.
- God I love sex, something that I want everyone to appreciate to the same degree. Get out there and get laid! Grab your sexuality by the ovaries! Tell him what to do, show him pleasure like he has never seen, and break the windows with your screaming orgasm(s)!! Hooking up with someone new is such a pleasure; enjoy it as much as you can!

Actions:

Like I said before this is the chapter of action. Hopefully we have held your hand and explained enough to help you hit the ground running. You may think that this is such a huge mountain to climb but I think you will be shocked at how quickly your life will change and your confidence explode. Just remember that you will have some unpleasant things happen but this is part of the journey and the mistakes can be just as enjoyable as the successes.

1. Once again if you didn't complete the list of how you can transform your life, how can you expect to act on anything we have asked you to do? Go finish that list and create the person you wish to be in order to raise your energy, improve your life, and draw a man that kicks as much ass as you do!

2. Getting back into the dating is going to take some of time from your life. Improving yourself will take a TON of time but the trade off is incredibly worth it. How can you cut the clutter/fat from your life? Here is another great time to make a list, ask yourself. What are the biggest time Suckers in my life? Facebook? Overtime? Crappy friends? TV? It is time to do a spring-cleaning on yourself, get rid of the garbage and fill that precious time with the person you have always wanted to become.

3. Figure out what your strategy is going to be, are you open to frivolous sex? Need to be a little more contained? Maybe you should just try it and see how you feel? I find just getting out there and having a good time will erase a lot of the pain in the past. Maybe this is not you and you just want to date without the sex? Just be prepared for negative consequences with either route but if you are, at a minimum, moving forward you will eventually arrive.

4. I know this sounds silly but go out and prepare for an encounter now. Get some condoms, put them in your purse, need a little lube with that? You may not use these for a while but this does two things. It prepares your mind for what is inevitable and it also insures that you are

prepared, when in a moment of weakness, you find yourself naked again.

5. Going to do this online? Put your toes in the water with the free service plentyoffish.com Create a profile according to Kim's advice. Now see what happens, as the assholes come out of the woodwork increase the assertiveness of your profile to filter out the morons. Go on a mini date with a couple, see how it goes. No good success here? Time to go for a paid service, from what I understand the paid sites bring much better quality men. Also there are a ton of books specifically on online dating, maybe you should educate yourself how to find a digital keeper. Oh... and... NO LDRs!!! (Long distance relationships)

6. Do you have your exit strategies? Nothing is more unpleasant than being stuck with someone unpleasant; don't underestimate how important this is.

7. Look in the mirror right now and tell yourself that you rock, you have a ton more relationship experience than most of people you are going to initially meet. You have been around the block and this time around you are going to do so much better. So go out and kick some ass!

Part four: Avoidance

We wanted to include this chapter since even though we are both experts in this we find we make the same mistakes. All of need to have drummed into our heads what not to do and although I would like to focus mainly on the positive we to self correct we need to be aware of the negative. Some of these things we have addressed before but like I said if we still step in these steaming cow pies of mistake, you certainly will too. Hopefully with your eyes a little more open it won't have to happen more than once.

IXV. Please stop! – Most common mistakes

The most common things tons of women Think/Do/Say WRONG when dating again.

Sex talk - "I feel so strange dating again! I haven't had sex since my ex-husband!" Okay baby seal... Do you really want to get clubbed that badly? This screams to any man that you don't know what the hell you are doing and he might as well put you out of your misery. It is imperative that you sit back and observe before you share your every emotion. He makes you excited and horny on the first date? NO! Slap your hands and keep your mouth shut! You are a newbie again and I don't care how much you want to say something sexual... you keep yourself as reserved as possible until you feel confident as a player again!

Ex talk - Remember in high school that one guy you would always complain to about your boyfriend? Remember how you kinda sorta knew that the only reason he put up with your complaining was because he was madly in love with you? Well, it was inappropriate then, and it is inappropriate now. Sure...it is very important to get your feelings off your chest, to let that emotion out so you don't explode but NOT WITH HIM! This is something that a lot of women don't understand: guys don't talk like girls. We are doers/fixers not listeners/empathizers. Have this kind of talk with your mom and/or a female friend but don't bring it up to him. (Unless he is madly in love with you and you just don't give a shit)

I don't want to waste time on assholes - Gawd... I hate hearing this. So many women getting back into dating again want some sort of quick magical fix for their dilemma. It just doesn't work that way, if you want to lose weight we both know it takes education and application. Dating is no different, and if you approach it with the wrong mindset you are bound to get frustrated that you have to meet so many idiots first. Resign yourself to the fact that dating again is a learning curve and it is going to be tough but fun. Look at it this way, the first time you strap on a snowboard you are going to have a sore ass but was it really a bad experience? No, because every other time you go out things are going to get better. Can you speed up this process? Yes! Dive in! Don't pull back out of fear, go break a friggin metaphorical dating bone or two. "Wasting time" is another way to say LEARNING, now enjoy the good with the "bad".

Where is this going talk - A lot of newly single women want to replace what they have lost ASAP whether that was a husband or stable long term boyfriend. Their house burnt down and all they can think about it building the comfort back up again. THIS IS A MISTAKE! This kind of negative crap about not wanting to waste time, or needing to rush the relationship only has the opposite effect. Take your time! Kiss some frogs! Expect a level of failure! This is normal and honestly it is fun. What is the best part of a tree-house, sitting in it or building it?

Focusing on the body/life you used to have verses the one you have - My closest female friend back in

Santa Barbara started out cutting my hair. We got along very well and eventually hung out, she liked me and I thought she was cool. About halfway into our "date" she pulled out pictures of her daughter. This was okay since I asked to see. As she pulled out the picture another picture fell out of petite grinning very young cute girl. "Wow, what a cutie, is this one of your sisters?" As I looked up at her I realized my mistake. "Thanks... That was me three years ago." I smiled, laughed and apologized. She looked about 10 years older and heavily worn with stress. "I know, I look like shit, being married, having a kid and going through divorce just destroys your body and your life."

Now please understand that I was attracted to Lacy, just the way she was. Sure I noticed she had a bit of junk in the trunk but I was cool with that. After she started to talk negatively about her body I started to reflect her emotion. I started to notice the things she complained about, and I became a little fearful of one day removing her clothing. Maybe under the clothes was a pile of skin jello some how molded into the shape of a woman by duct tape and super glue?

Negative self-talk will never ever get you anywhere with any man, unless he is a life coach and takes you on as a project! (Which I was ironically) Don't put a spotlight on your flaws (but telling him you're missing an arm is necessary disclosure) since what you may think of as a flaw is probably a non-issue for him.

This is the body/life you have right now and to dislike it is a sure way to get more of what you dislike. If you wish to change, you first must accept/forgive/love your body, you know this is true, right?

Projecting on to all men the pain of your divorce - When I first started my blog I had a significant number of single mommy bloggers stop by. Every once in a while something I wrote would trigger some pain. This is what one mommy blogger wrote in response to a post I wrote on responsibility for the type of partner you are currently getting.

"I'm having a hard time here, because I have the need to stand up and yell BULLSHIT as loud as I can. And trust me when I say, I'm not a needy chick.
I hate hate hate that you started one of your paragraphs with Why you are responsible. I refuse to believe this. I don't tell a man I'm going to call when I'm not interested in him. I don't lead him to believe I'm into him and then run in the other direction. I don't play games. I refuse to believe that I'm responsible for a man being too much of a chicken shit to give me the simple act of telling me the truth ... He's Just Not That Into Me!"

Do you feel the anger emanating here? Can you imagine being the guy dating her? He would be terrified to tell her the truth and thus fulfill her claim that men are cowardly, game playing, and chicken shits. Where does this belief come from? Is it rooted from a past relationship, possibly the man that just left her?

This very angry woman is going to get the same results over and over and over again because she is projecting a belief on men that is self-fulfilling. I believe that this is an enormous problem that many recently divorce women share. They feel horribly injured after separation and project that fear and mistrust on to ALL MEN. This is just as bad as my father saying, "Mike, there are blacks and then there are N...." I find this a horribly offensive stereotype and I am shocked that my very kind, wise father still has Detroit racism in his blood. I make this point not to offend but to open your eyes to

179

the possibility that you might be just as bad. Did a dog bite you once? Are all dogs bad? Got mugged in New York? Is New York bad? Dated a guy that cheated on you? Are all men cheaters? Obviously, NO...

Not only is a thought process like this very very damaging but like I said above it is something your brain will start to seek out in order to prove it's view of the world is correct. How does my father reinforce his skewed views? He watches sports and adores the black athletes, then he watches COPs and shakes his head sagely. (Not noticing that the arresting officer is black.) Want to find a bunch of really crappy guys to treat you really crappy? First assume that they are crappy and you will receive what you asked for without fail.

Going to bed with him too soon - It is kinda funny but a lot of women I have seen recently divorce or get out of long term monogamous relationships, go a little slutty for a while. While this is healing in some ways it is also a bit of a problem, since the guy usually doesn't stick around. It was true 30 years ago and it is true now. You do him too soon and he may not stick around long enough to even get to know you.

Not a ton of explaining to do here since you already know not to sleep with a man too soon and no amount of my begging or cajoling will convince you otherwise. You just need to get burned a few times before you realize that this is not the result you want.

I am not asking you to be prudish, I am asking you to be patient. Men respect this patience if they respect you and the men that don't? Fuck em! (not literally!). Use your sexual will power as a human coffee filter, drink the yummy coffee and put the grounds in the garbage.

A little reminder!

When to do the deed:
- When you truly feel his sincerity (careful here, your genitals might be urging you to slip into a lie)
- After, no less then 3-4 "real" dates (no meeting him at Starbucks on his lunch break doesn't count)
- You have been to second base a few times! (Same night doesn't count!)
- He doesn't seem obsessed with sleeping with you and puts on ZERO pressure
- You just can't resist anymore!!!

When NOT to do the deed:
- He bought you a really nice dinner and you feel the need to reciprocate
- WOW... it is the first date! And this might be the ONE!
- OMG he is hot, if I don't get him now he may not come back!
- He seems irritated that you won't put out (BIG warning sign that he only wants sex)

Talk about the Ex - Girl, don't even go there - Ladies, ladies, ladies. There are so many good and wonderful things to say in the presence of a man you are dating...why say something that could totally ruin the fun?!

Telling your date what a douchebag your ex is, probably will translate what a douchebag **HE** is. Men have extraordinarily large egos. Don't give him any reason to think you will EVER deflate his!

181

I think Mike will agree with me that there is absolutely no reason to bring up your ex unless someone asks about him. And, yeah, usually they'll ask. But we'll deal with that later. Right now I want to talk about what NOT to say in a dating situation. Read this carefully. If you've seen yourself in some of these scenarios don't feel bad, brush it off and remember NEVER to do it again!

Yes I agree 1000%, talking about your ex is the same as talking about a horrible experience. You relive it right in front of him and you simply look ugly and unattractive.

No Marriage Talk - Don't talk about how you're ready to get married, what are you trying to do scare him off? Have him go running for the hills? Men typically view marriage as a trap until they find someone they wouldn't mind being in that trap with. Let him bring it up...about two years after you've been dating!

"Men chase women until she catches him. Don't go the other direction."

Don't laugh at him...do it at home - Don't tell your date he obviously doesn't understand relationships since he's never been married. Okay, yeah, I know his longest relationship lasted 6 months, and he was backpacking across Europe for most of that...but don't belittle him and remind him of his lack of maturity or ability to commit. Just nod and smile if he ever says such an asinine term as "I want my marriage to be just like my grandparents who wouldn't even utter the word divorce" and laugh your ass off at home when you think about his grandparents not having had sex in 30 of the 50 years they've dared not utter the word divorce!

My Ex was hot in the sack - Don't talk about all the great sex you and the ex had. Do I really need to explain? Okay, just because you asked nicely: you talk about the great sex you and hubby had, equals current date wondering if your ex is bigger and better than him. If in your case the answer is yes, make sure your dates will never know that!

I miss him - Don't talk about how much you miss your ex-dude, you got divorced for a reason! Either you don't mind missing him that much or he's not missing you all that much. No man (or woman) wants to hear about how you miss your ex. No One.

We never had sex - Your date is automatically thinking: "It's always the woman's fault if a man doesn't want to have sex with you. Because a man will have sex with just about anyone/anything. So, what's wrong with you and I don't want to end up like her ex!"
Or your date will take his thought in the exact opposite direction:
"She and her ex did have sex...she just wanted a lot more of it. What is she, some kind of man-eating nympho? I can't keep up with that! I don't even want to try. I'll go find a girl w/ a "normal" sex drive that I can live up to and won't expect super human sex from me!"
You really may have never had enough sex with your ex but don't utter these words to a man...remember, in their minds it's always the woman's fault!

You didn't want the divorce - Your date is thinking, "He wanted the divorce, she's flawed." "He left her for a younger and prettier woman, which is why she didn't want the divorce and he did, because she's flawed! Well if he didn't want her, why should I?"

I hate to say it but Kim is dead on, if you are the one that is left, it makes you look like someone's cast offs.

183

That is not a very attractive thing; no one wants what is rejected by others.

Men are scum and can't be trusted :
- "I don't know why anyone would ever get married" - He's thinking "... to you!"
- "Yeah I really stuck it to him with the alimony/child support/got the house and dog!" - This woman is just out for my hard earned money. She did it to the last guy (she even got the dog!) she'll do it to me too!

Yes you are a mega bitch in his mind and he will probably execute is exit strategy and never call you again!

It blows my mind but Kim has an important point here. I have had many girls communicate to me how much they dislike men. Ah... hello??? Have you noticed that I might be a guy? Want me to talk about what bitches women are?

Wrap up

There are so many mistakes that you can make and we can't cover everything here but this is part of the learning process we keep talking about. Make mistakes, ask questions, stay optimistic, and allow yourself to move closer to your goal.

XV. Should you introduce the Kids??

I don't have kids but I can tell you how a lot of single men feel about a woman that has them and it isn't as cut as dry as you might think.

Your three lovely boys

I agree they are really lovely but unless he has 3 very lovely girls and wants to re-enact the Brady Bunch, you might have just scared the crap out of him.

When I was on Plenty Of Fish recently, I was contacted by a 24-year-old girl with 5 kids. (She also worked at McDonalds) On her profile she had her kids in all of her pictures appearing to suckle off of her like a mother sow. Her perfect date? "We would have a nice dinner with the kids, I would put them to bed and we would snuggle on the couch and watch a movie." I swear, this is no joke! After cleaning the vomit out of my goatee, I saw the humor in this and was fascinated by my own revulsion.

I hate to say it but he most likely doesn't have stellar feelings towards another man's children. In fact this very often is a deal breaker, UNLESS he is eased into the idea. I have dated women with kids and recently took one of them very seriously, not to mention I adored her children! What was the difference? She didn't put her kids on parade. She wasn't apologetic about it and she showed me that she could have a life beyond her children. I liked this, and found myself wanting to get to know her children since they were not thrust in my face.

Upshot? Don't put pictures of your kids on your online profile OR talk about them unless he asks. Don't be apologetic of your kids and DON'T use them to disqualify men. Do have a separate life beyond your children and do trust that he will accept them as he has accepted you. Kids are scary for guys, proceed with caution but do proceed. We will talk a little bit more about this later.

Ladies, I know that Mike sounds awfully raw here but you need to listen to him. Mike is a very kind empathetic guy but he knows himself well enough to be ridiculously honest. This is truly for your benefit and something that you need to understand but don't let it get you down! If it is done right, I am sure even Mike would be happy to be a wonderful step-father.

Thanks Kim, and yes you are right

Here is a question I got from a reader that might help you understand more.

Question: When do I tell my date I have kids? - Sarah in Arizona

A: Great question Sarah! First things first. If you made this guy's acquaintance on the wonderful world wide web he should know that you have kids. Unfortunately, some men are dufuses and don't fully read your profile. I've been known to sit down to dinner with a man, casually mention something about my boys and get a look of shock that comes across their face. Uh, did you know that I'm divorced? No? Did you know that I'm

186

black? A woman? But back to you Sarah. Tell them right away, if you meet online, casually question if they saw you have kids on the profile. You: "You saw that I have children, right?" If you meet in person, no need to tell them until the first date. A casual question like "Do you have any kids?" Let them answer and then respond to your own question. Easy peasy.

Kim, I would like to add to your add really quick. Yes, tell him you have kids but then leave it there. Let him inquire about this area of your life, don't volunteer. It sounds a little rough but very few men consider it a plus that you have had children unless they have their own. Be cautious here. **Understand that he needs to care about you first before he can care about your kids.**

Video: When to introduce the kids?
http://www.startdatingagain.net/?page_id=60
Kim and Mike differ a bit in their opinion on when to introduce the kids. Dangerous topic and one hopefully we can help you understand more.

XVI. Talking about the Ex

If you haven't started dating yet, good job for buying this book when you did! If you've dated as much as I have (and that's quite a lot!) you know that this question comes up often. Most men look at me and wonder how the hell anyone so smart, successful, and stunning could not have a man. Some men wonder, some men ask out loud. You have one of two options:

1. I'd rather not talk about it right now
2. We just grew apart

This response was built off of an observation Mike made that I think would be helpful to share. Before writing this book when asked why I was divorced I would reply with:

"He started fooling around with a co-worker, but wanted to keep me as the perfect wife. I told him only if I could have a boy-toy on the side." When Mike read what wrote he stated that he didn't feel I was being very sincere and it felt more like a cover-up of some serious pain.

OUCH...

I must admit Mike hit the nail right on the head. I wasn't being sincere and this reply was covering up the pain. Just like Mike saw through my answer about my breakup and divorce, others will see through yours, if bitterness, pain or resentment still resides. Remember you are not obligated to go into great detail or even explain to a date about past relationships. Reserve that for if the relationship grows in time.

As I'm writing this, a rush of emotion welled up inside me and tears started to fall. I tell you this to let you realize that though you are moving on and changing for the better is perfectly normal to mourn the relationship you once had and treasured. Cry, scream, mourn, and get it out of your system in private so when you present your face to the world- and especially to the men you date- you are confident and whole.

Let me reiterate! NO Dissin' the Ex

Sometimes now I use a simple "We just grew apart. Great guy, great father, I wish him well." This shows that you hold no hard feelings and you are above the pettiness that was probably inflicted upon you during your break up.

I don't care why you and your ex couldn't make it to your 50th wedding anniversary... don't go dissin' him. No bad talk about the ex, even if he was a serial killer or stole candy from babies. Know why? Because the cute date sitting across from you at dinner is measuring your "bat shit crazy" factor. You know, if you could potentially be the crazy girl who calls him 50 times in one day to demand where he is and who he's sleeping with or if you're really just interested in a large financial payout.

He's wondering how you could love someone enough to commit or marry him, and then tear him apart to a perfect stranger when things went wrong. He's mentally adding up how you will react in the likelihood of you two dating, sleeping together, or having a committed relationship.

Measuring Up

If you bash your ex, brag about the divorce settlement, or declare loudly that you hope his dick falls off and the mistress he cheated on you with gets syphilis in her left eye...well, he's not really going to look towards a second date with you.

I've also had many dates ask me what my ex does for a living. Mike has really helped me out with this one. I believe it has to do with the competitiveness of being a man. I've heard that men measure their penises and check each other out in the shower to see who's member is larger. I'm guessing this is the same thing as it pertains to career and money made.

Your date wants to see if he's good enough for you or if you're a gold digger. Mike tells me it's also a qualifier. If a man asks this he wants to know what your standard is, what you're used to. I guess it depends on the guy. Since your Divorce Guru is always fly, well dressed and in 5 inch heels on a date, lives in a hip neighborhood, and has two kids, I'm guessing my dates that have asked want to know if they will be obligated to provide the same lifestyle that my ex appears to have provided for me. I subtly let them know that I work hard and have lofty, crazy goals...i.e. you're not expected foot the bills for my manicures or my boys private school tuition. I want to pay my own way. It's nice if you want to buy me a Mercedes, but that's definitely on my own to do list!

He's Wondering: Are you a gold digger?

Maybe this isn't your thing. Maybe your ex was a doctor and you want someone who has the cash, can keep you in a summer house, and fur coats. Maybe your ex was a janitor and you want your next guy to have money. I don't care if you're a gold digger or not, just don't appear that way for your dates. No man wants to be seen as a meal ticket or as the way out of your tiny apartment and Ford Fiesta. Remember, no bashing or bragging about the amount (or lack of) money your ex makes. So keep it vague ladies, it really isn't his business anyway.

I think it really comes down to this, just don't do it. Have a nice canned answer or just tell him you would rather talk about happier subjects. Even I have to remind myself of this but ironically I love all of my exes still! So when I bring them up, girls get quite uncomfortable. Sigh… best just to avoid the topic, good or bad.

XVII. Conclusion - Ready to get in the game!

I once heard an 80-year-old Canadian author explain her lovely secret to happiness. It had three simple parts:

1. Something to do
2. Someone to love
3. Someone to love you

I thought this was so simple and elegantly true. This really is all we need and men have these needs as much as women do. I want to stress that this book is not about replacing that void in your life but it is a stepping-stone to get you at least two of the three needs listed above.

I hope that I can encourage you to get back out there. To not see the dating world as dangerous, but a fun adventure place!

It is so exciting what is in front of you. There are so many new people to interact with and new networks to create. There are TONS new people to fall in and out of love with! Wonderful pain and Joy, life's sweet and sour combination. You are about to enter a new stage in life and I am excited for you. I have no doubt that the second time around you will have much better results than you did the first. Life is about growth and I am excited and jealous of your journey.

BTW don't hesitate to make a mistake with me if you get a chance. I will be the cute single guy with the light brown hair, don't hesitate to say hi.

I conclude with attitude

Everything changes. Life is change. You wouldn't be reading this if things never changed. My relationship with my ex changed. Your relationship with your ex has changed. Change is inevitable, and I know it can be for the good.

Major change can sometimes be hard, heartbreaking, and physically exhausting. What makes the difference in how this change affects your life better or worse is attitude.

"The longer I live, the more I realize the impact of attitude on life. Attitude, to me, is more important than facts. It is more important than the past, the education, the money, than circumstances, than failure, than successes, than what other people think or say or do. It is more important than appearance, giftedness or skill. It will make or break a company... a church... a home. The remarkable thing is we have a choice everyday regarding the attitude we will embrace for that day. We cannot change our past... we cannot change the fact that people will act in a certain way. We cannot change the inevitable. The only thing we can do is play on the one string we have, and that is our attitude. I am convinced that life is 10% what happens to me and 90% of how I react to it. And so it is with you... we are in charge of our Attitudes." - Charles R. Swindoll

I filed for divorce and began dealing with strenuous court cases involving child custody and restraining orders against the man I once adored. I moved out of my 20th floor downtown apartment with the view of the bay and sublet a room in a tiny railroad apartment. This sublet was only for one month and after that I didn't know where I was going to live. I had no money, my boys had to live with their dad, and I had no job. My life had radically changed within a matter of weeks and I did not know what the future held for me.

This is where the impact of attitude on life came in handy. I had the attitude that everything would be alright. I persisted in having hope and faith. I ended up taking a part time job at Starbucks, a far cry from the political and government jobs I had once had, and was miraculously approved for an affordable and cute apartment in a great neighborhood that was big enough for my two boys and me. I woke up in the morning sometimes exhausted, sometimes happy to be starting a new life- but always with the positive mindset that all I could do is "play on the one string" that I had which was my attitude.

Today, as I write this book, I still adamantly advocate that your attitude is what directs your life. When I began dating after my divorce I had the attitude that I wasn't good enough. So I attracted men who treated me like I wasn't good enough. Once I changed my attitude about myself, I almost instantly started attracting men who treated me like I was doing them a favor by spending time with them, a vastly different result for a small change in attitude.

Have the attitude that you deserve fun, exciting dates. Have the attitude that love is available to you. Have the attitude that you are worthy of a sexy, fulfilling life and this is what you'll receive. The change that I have gone through since my divorce has been rough but has caused a growth and strength in me that I had no idea was possible.

Henry Kissinger once said, "A diamond is a chunk of coal that is made good under pressure." This quote so speaks to change that can be stressful and hard because diamonds are formed when extreme heat and pressure cause carbon atoms to crystallize. The process is painful but what you get when it's over is beautiful, sparkling, and strong. Have the attitude that your break up or divorce is the extreme heat and pressure that will one day make you even stronger and more beautiful.

My roommate who I shared the sublet with for a month after I filed for divorce, gave me the above quote on attitude by Charles R. Swindoll. I remember coming home discouraged from a crappy day of serving coffee, mopping gross floors and $34 in the bank to see and read this quote lying on my bed with a flower. I instantly started crying out of relief and joy that someone cared about me enough to pass along such great wisdom. Just like someone cared about me, Mike and I write this book to let you know that we care for you and want you to live a happy dating life that will one day lead to loving again.

Know that the best is yet to come.

Sincerely,

Kim Hess and Mike Masters

Did you like this book? Help us spread the word on Amazon and get the word out to more people that need help moving back into the relationship game!

The link to our Amazon Page: http://www.amazon.com/Ex-Next-Empowered-Breakup-ebook/dp/B003UV8N64

Thank you!

Both Mike Masters and Kim Hess are available for coaching you back into the relationship game. Feel free to contact Kim at khdivorceguru@gmail.com or Mike Masters at mikethemasterdater@gmail.com

Send your general questions to backintherelationshipgame@gmail.com

Made in the USA
Lexington, KY
08 November 2011